VIOLENCE IN YOUR WORKPLACE

To Debbie,

Who knows that
most of us have
a choice as to
whether we are
victims or not!

All my love,

[signature]

July 1994

By the same author

MARTIAL ARTS FOR PEOPLE WITH DISABILITIES
An Introduction

HUMAN HORIZONS SERIES

VIOLENCE IN YOUR WORKPLACE

How to Cope

Dirk Robertson

drawings by Dorette Hibbert

A CONDOR BOOK
SOUVENIR PRESS (E&A) LTD

First published 1993 by Souvenir Press (Educational & Academic) Ltd, 43 Great Russell Street, London WC1B 3PA and simultaneously in Canada

ISBN 0 285 63153 5

Photoset by Rowland Phototypesetting Ltd, Bury St Edmunds, Suffolk and printed in Great Britain by St Edmundsbury Press Ltd, Bury St Edmunds, Suffolk

To Bruspa and Vittoria

Foreword

Every year countless numbers of people are assaulted in one way or another during the course of their work. Whilst this can happen to people in all walks of life, it is particularly common towards those who deal with the public— social workers, nurses, police officers and the men and women who work in our nation's transport system.

It is no coincidence that all these professions involve contact with people who may be feeling highly stressed, aggrieved, vulnerable or who consider themselves the victims of social injustice. Violence is all too often the result of people passing the boiling point, then taking it out on those nearest to them.

As a former social worker myself, I know what it is like to be faced with threatened and actual violence and, more importantly, I have been given well-meaning advice about how to cope, which has never seemed to take into account the reality of my working situation.

At last a book which is practical, informative and, above all, realistic, both in terms of the advice offered and in the range of problems covered. No one condones violence, but Dirk Robertson bravely shows that people have a right to defend themselves, to maintain their physical and emotional well-being and, most importantly, a right not to be assaulted or injured whilst working for the benefit of others.

The book is simply, clearly and concisely set out, refreshingly clear of jargon and firmly focused on the important and relevant facts on the subject of violence. Where physical options of defence are suggested, the illustrations show exactly what is meant and how to execute the proposed techniques. Balanced with this are well thought-out chapters which consider the problems of violence and possible non-physical responses.

Especially valuable is the way in which the book considers the make-up of individuals' personalities and the reality that some types of option involving aggression and specific physical action as a response to violence are not appropriate because some people are just not capable of being violent themselves. Dirk Robertson does not forget this, and for that and the fact that this is not just another 'self-defence' book I wholeheartedly recommend it as a valuable addition to everyone's bookshelf. It is already on mine, for you never know when or where you are going to have to respond to violence in your workplace!

David Hinchliffe, MP
Labour Spokesman on the Personal Social Services
and Community Care

Publisher's Note

The author and publishers are not responsible in any manner for any injury which may occur by reading and/or following any instructions, advice or suggestions in this book.

If you are going to take any course of action which involves strenuous physical activity, medical advice should always be sought in the first instance.

Contents

Acknowledgements

My thanks to Dorette Hibbert for her drawings, Roy Victor for the cover photograph, Yuk-King and. for their continued support, advice and enthusiasm, my publishers.

For permission to quote from published material I am grateful to *Community Care* for their issue of 25 March 1993, Macmillan Magazines for *Social Work Today* of 2 November 1989, BASW for *Practice* Vol. 1 No. 3, Hertfordshire Social Services for their 'Staff Guidelines on Violence by Clients', and UNISON for the NALGO 'Violence at Work Paper', 1992. The quotation from *British Crime Survey 1988* by Pat Mayhew, David Elliott and Lizanne Dowds, Home Office Research Study no. 111, is Crown Copyright, reproduced with the permission of the Controller of Her Majesty's Stationery Office.

I would also especially like to thank Lydia Burton, who is always so ready to lend a hand.

Introduction

Violence, even the mere mention of the word, can make the most confident and secure person freeze completely, or shake with seemingly no control over his or her emotions. Violence in the workplace is not a joke.

The after-effects can be equally devastating: constant brooding over what happened, fear and doubt about the events leading up to the incident and, in many cases, a complete or partial loss of self-esteem which may have serious side-effects for the rest of one's life.

Sometimes violence comes without warning, at others it is the consequence of built-up frustration or a sequence of aggressive actions which the victim may feel powerless to avert. There are self-defence courses and there is a wealth of ready advice about what to do when confronted with violence or the possibility of it, but what the courses and advice often fail to take into account is the individual personalities of the people concerned and their attitudes to aggression and violence. Not only that: the one vital factor which is generally ignored is that few people will be able to enjoy the luxury of not dealing with the consequences of their responses to violence threatened against them.

Nowhere is this truer than in the caring or helping professions. If you are threatened or faced with violence, then, almost invariably, just lashing out to defend yourself is not only out of step with your professional guidelines but probably out of character as well. The sad truth remains, however, that there may come a time when you are required to defend yourself, in one way or another, if you are to avoid serious injury or even death.

For many people this nightmare has already come frighteningly true: 'More than two-thirds of all council staff in Bexley who suffered violent attacks over a three month period worked in social services,' reported *Community Care* magazine on 25 March 1993. Bexley had carried out a survey between October and December 1992, which showed that the majority of these attacks were on residential social workers and care assistants. One pregnant worker was actually struck in the stomach.

This is not just a recent development. In its issue of 2 November 1989

Social Work Today noted: 'Soaring violence figures in Notts childrens' homes. Monitoring of violence towards staff in the social services department has revealed 524 incidents took place last year with 260 occurring in the county's twenty-six children's homes.'

Newspaper reports, television programmes and public opinion all seem to suggest that violence has increased in a most dramatic fashion. But for many people who work in direct contact with the public, particularly in social work, nursing, health care, police, transport and so on, it has always been there. Individuals who are already frustrated, angry or desperate, or who feel powerless, can be very aggressive, even violent, towards those very people who are attempting to provide them with a service.

If you are one of these people, then this book is for you. Indeed, if you are unsure how to deal with violence when you are confronted by it, regardless of whether you work in a profession which gives you direct contact with the public, then there may be something here of benefit to you as well.

I could provide a wealth of facts and figures from the various professions mentioned above, but this book is not intended to be a statistical analysis of the information available on the subject. It is an attempt to offer something concrete to people who have faced violence, who may face it in the future or who are unsure exactly how they might react in the face of aggression and violence from people whom they may be trying to help.

Any suggestion that one should respond to problems in a physical way will always result in argument and controversy. I accept that not everyone holds the same view about what is and is not appropriate. Moreover, there are some who say that, no matter what happens, there can be no excuse or justification for responding physically.

Whilst I respect this view, and the right of people to hold it, I think that, unfortunately, there are times when, if you are not prepared to take certain steps to protect yourself or maintain your safety, there is a very real chance that you will not be in a fit condition to continue your work, or provide for your family, or whatever your main activity or contribution to your immediate environment may be. You yourself may choose never to hurt anyone or to cause them distress or pain, but others may not live by the same code, or in times of distress may be incapable of discerning right from wrong.

There are whole areas of work that can bring you into contact with expected or unexpected aggression and violence. Obviously, you can plan for the expected or the probable, but it is far more difficult to be prepared for behaviour that is unexpected.

If you are a nurse working in a section of health care which commonly exposes you to verbal and physical violence, you may know the situations which you must be ready to tackle, but the most common perception amongst the general public is that, in health care, aggression and violence are mainly experienced by those who work with the mentally ill or with psychiatric in-patients.

This is simply not the case. There is no evidence to link mental illness, in general, with violence. The popular view of hospital wards catering for the mentally ill is of white-clad 'inmates' stalking the corridors ready to explode at the slightest provocation. Really this is probably a more accurate description of a Friday night accident and emergency department, with the tell-tale smell of alcohol in the air. Violence can and does occur in those sections of nursing commonly associated with it, but generally professionals in those fields are more prepared and trained with this specific aspect in mind.

Likewise in social work, the popular notion of violence is associated with large adolescents doing what they like and beating up anyone who gets in their way. To a certain extent this unfortunate scenario has an element of truth, but violence is also rife in the care of the elderly, which many people may find surprising or even unbelievable. Punching, kicking, hair-pulling, attacks with weapons with the intent to endanger life and limb—these experiences are all too common for many carers whose work brings them into direct contact with elderly people. In *Practice*, Vol. 1 No. 3: Violence to Staff, Norman Tutt notes that 'staff in residential care for the elderly are at greatest risk'. Again, it is a great shame that people should behave like that, and also it is entirely appropriate to explain such behaviour in terms of dementia, memory loss or the whole range of terminology used to describe the human condition in the twilight years.

But descriptions, analyses, suggestions of root problems do not in themselves provide tangible support in dealing face-to-face with the results of the human condition. They can and do establish the arena for discussion, learning, sharing of information and the creation of a body of knowledge associated with individual types of 'cases', but they have failed to address in detail such questions as what people should do when confronted with the consequences of another's individual condition or frustration.

Far too many researchers, statisticians and theorists in the field of human welfare do not work in direct contact with the people they are talking about. It is almost as though there were two worlds: the one which is talked about and the one which is worked in. On the many full- and part-time courses I have attended over the years, aggression and violence have always been referred to as 'avoidable problems'. If you, as a worker, look at your own actions and the way in which you conduct yourself, and have a greater understanding of what it is like to be a 'client', then that will more or less solve the problems of violence and aggression from people you are supposed to be caring for.

For a time, a very short one, I actually believed this. Whenever I witnessed aggression and violence towards workers I automatically assumed that they were at fault, and when I myself was exposed to aggression and violence I would sit for hours going over it again and again, trying to work out what I had done or said to provoke this situation.

But the simple truth is that, no matter how thoughtful or careful you may be, if someone else decides that you are going to be the focus of his or her frustration, whether expressed verbally or physically, then often it is not actually your fault.

Obviously it is useful to understand the causes and contributory factors that lead to human violence, and studying the theories and background on human nature can offer a great deal towards the understanding, care and compassion that one person gives to another. But in the field of human welfare, without practical support and advice the theories often lead nowhere.

Whilst there may be similarities in people's behaviour in certain situations, every individual is different. It is difficult if not impossible to say what each person will do in a particular case, and the same person may behave and react completely differently in situations which, on the surface, appear similar. This factor alone can make working with people unpredictable and requires a flexible, open and, if possible, relaxed attitude which ultimately can lead to increased safety both for yourself and your colleagues.

I know it is not always that easy, in work settings, since people assume roles that may be at variance with their attributes or character. This problem is also linked to gender and race, which we shall be examining in chapter 1.

My main reason for writing this book is because I have been there: I have stood rooted to the spot in the face of both verbal aggression and physical violence, with sweaty palms and trembling legs, and wondered, 'What do I do next?'

The next step is basically dictated by who you are, what you care about and what you are trying to achieve in terms of the best possible outcome, and all this lumped together means that you have a range of possible choices, some appropriate, some inappropriate. When you are the one who is faced with the aggression and/or violence the choice is yours, but the consequences may affect not only you but other people as well, and if you are working in a public-orientated profession that is not something you can ignore or put to one side.

Taking everything into consideration, the question 'What do I do next?' is neither simple nor straightforward, and whilst this book is not intended to provide all the answers it may help light the way for you to see, as an individual, what you can and cannot do in the name of self-preservation and perhaps, more importantly, what you are and are not prepared to do.

1 What You Need to Know

It is very important to understand that fear robs you of approximately seventy per cent of your oxygen. So immediately you are only working with thirty per cent of your usual amount of air in your lungs. We shall be looking at ways of counteracting this later in the book, when we deal with the practical issues of self-preservation.

I met a social worker who had been abducted when she went to visit a client. He taped a shotgun to her head and then forced her to drive around the county for half a day before it all ended 'peacefully'. But for the social worker there was no peace: she still goes over the ordeal again and again, in her head, thinking, 'What could I have done differently?' 'What did I do wrong?'

A residential social worker is one who works shifts and sleeps in an establishment where the recipients of the service actually live, like a children's home. One residential social worker asked a young person to go to bed at a certain time, and without warning had three of his teeth knocked out and his orbital bone (around the eye) fractured, requiring plastic surgery to rebuild the support for the eye. He left the job convinced that it was his fault and that there was no future for him in the caring professions if 'that was the effect he had on people'. On one occasion, when I visited him, he was so depressed he wouldn't answer the door.

There are more stories, enough to fill the book on their own. It is possible that, while you are reading this, some similar experience may spring to mind. Obviously there are instances when someone's behaviour or approach to a problem in dealing with the public is inappropriate, and may result in the escalation of aggression or violence from a client towards a worker. Specific training can often alleviate this problem by developing greater insight on the part of an individual worker who frequently experiences aggressive or violent reactions to his or her presence or involvement in someone's life.

But by far the greater number of people subjected to verbal and physical violence are victims of something which they do not understand or do not know how to deal with, and they find the experience very frightening and often professionally and personally demoralising.

There is a general belief that one cannot defend or protect oneself against physical or verbal abuse because the people who are the perpetrators are clients of a service. This is a terrible myth which has contributed to a situation in which people are afraid to look after themselves.

Think about it. If you are mentally or physically unable to do your job or to relate to people in a relaxed and confident way, then surely the clients and recipients of your services will suffer in the long run anyway. You thus owe it not just to yourself but to your clients to look after yourself and to protect yourself so that you will be there another day to provide for others, as well as yourself.

FEAR

This is the key to everything. We all fear something, even though certain people pretend to themselves and to others that nothing scares them, that they take life as it comes and that nothing bothers them. This is dangerous talk as it is invariably untrue, and if you start to believe that only people who are not 'scared' of anything are worth anything then your self-esteem and self-worth will start to suffer as you recognise your own constant and repetitive fears.

There is nothing to be ashamed of about being afraid. It is healthy, normal and universal. What varies is exactly what people are afraid of and how much they will admit.

I have a vivid and real memory of what happened in a social work office where I was working, when a child protection case came in. I was selected to accompany another social worker to confront a man with allegations of brutality perpetrated by him against members of his family.

My palms went dry, my tongue stuck to the roof of my mouth, I came out in a red-faced flush and my feet stayed firmly rooted to the floor. I was petrified of this man of violence and one thing was sure: I did not want to go to his house accusing him of terrible activities against his children.

Someone asked me what the matter was and I simply said, 'I'm scared!' There was a deathly hush in the office; you could have heard a pin drop. After what seemed like an age, a small voice from the corner of the room said, 'So am I'. 'And me,' said another. 'Yeah, me too!' chipped in another. Eventually the whole office admitted to complete and absolute fear and trepidation, not just in relation to this one case but to a whole range of different cases, in which the workers themselves felt vulnerable or at risk.

The important point was that no one had ever said they were scared and, even more significantly, no one had ever asked. Everyone presumed that he or she was the only one who felt fearful about the work we all had to do. There was an element of arrogance and egocentricity in this, in that we had each thought we were the only ones who were affected adversely—when in reality everyone around us felt sick!

The result of all these people, including myself, coming clean about how we really felt was, firstly, a clearing of the air, secondly, a common bonding of understanding that fear is not gender-specific, and, thirdly and most importantly, a realisation that you probably will not overcome it yourself if you try to deal with it alone, that you need other people to develop a strategy for coping and recognising quite natural fear in your everyday work contact with other human beings.

THE GENDER FACTOR

Gender roles play an integral part in the creation and maintenance of misconceptions about who should behave in a certain way and when. This is as true in the workplace as it is anywhere else and is particularly relevant when considering the caring professions such as social work.

Women are traditionally seen as compliant, co-operative and receptive to situations and problems and are sometimes only allowed to step out of that role when dealing in a professional capacity with other people's problems. A lot of men create this kind of environment, wittingly and unwittingly, in the workplace, and likewise a lot of women are forced into accepting it or colluding with it, since often this may appear the easiest option.

Ultimately, those who create this type of situation or collude with it are doing themselves and everyone near them a great disfavour, as stereotypical roles have a nasty habit of being very difficult to shake off once they have been thrust upon you, or you have been coerced into accepting them.

Once violence and aggression are entered into the equation in a work environment, it can be very unpleasant, even dangerous, for people to have conscious or subconscious gender roles which they suddenly find they are unable to break out of.

The classic image of a man is that of protector, provider and solver of problems, particularly of a physical nature. This strengthens the territorial aspect of the role. For example, a man at work would see the workplace as his 'territory' and place to be protected, and the people he worked with as being part of his group or clan rather than legitimate work colleagues. The result of this would be that any aggression or physical violence would have to be resolved in a way that showed the man as 'winning' and therefore protecting his territory.

This can be played out in an extremely conscious fashion or in a more subconscious way, to the extent that the people displaying this kind of behaviour do so without even realising it. Again, it is really a one-way street, as people will almost automatically look to such an individual to protect and provide, regardless of whether it is appropriate or not. This sort of scenario is

21

especially true in groups or teams which are predominantly female, with a male leader (particularly true in social services where women make up a large proportion of the regular workforce but a relatively small percentage of managers). The enforcement of such images and stereotypes can be addressed, and should be, in conventional team meetings and individual supervision. If you are a man and your role or behaviour is questioned or challenged by your colleagues, male or female, then the best thing you can do is listen and accept the possibility that you should look at your role and the way you present yourself.

This process is important as it is destructive and counter-productive for people to resent being questioned or challenged or given advice. The whole point of having a team is that everyone works together, allowing for the fact that someone is in charge. But there is an important difference between being in charge of people and being in charge of every situation. The one does not necessarily presuppose the other.

Likewise, if you are the one who is questioning or challenging someone else's way of presenting himself, it does no harm to be careful and precise in the way you tackle the subject. The relaxed and suggestive approach is more likely to bear fruit than the 'bull in a china shop' method. In addition, there is always the danger that, rather than being successful in getting someone to look at the way he behaves, you may just replace him as the all-powerful leader and solver of problems—a role which, I feel, no one can really fulfil but which many find themselves in for precisely the reasons we have looked at.

As well as actually taking the time to look at gender roles through meetings and supervision, meaningful and constructive inroads can be made step by step, in everyday situations at work. These can be as simple as not always having the women make the tea and the men sort out technical or electrical difficulties.

It is very important for women to have a collective voice in the workplace. Despite the popular and rather obnoxious image of females ganging up on helpless male victims in an office witch hunt, the reality is actually quite different. Men at work have an unfortunate habit of being quite 'clubby'. They, far more than women, have a tendency to group together in the face of a common enemy (like feminism in action), and attempt by fair means or foul to bring the situation under their control.

The result of this is that, if you are female and attempt to challenge or redress stereotypical roles which are thrust upon you, there is a distinct possibility that others (mainly men or women who do not want to upset the status quo) will do their best to make you appear like an obsessed and ardent feminist who is unable to leave her 'political' views at home, where they belong.

Resist this with all your might, as a group. It is far more difficult for work colleagues to isolate you if you have a common view and a clear, concise way of presenting it.

At the same time do not be lured into the role of 'superwoman', which is quite common. If you are unprepared to accept traditional restricting views of women, then one of the common strategies to isolate you is to label and identify you as some kind of 'Amazon' expert in unarmed combat, jungle warfare and urban survival, not to mention a brilliant cook. This is unfair and unjust but very easy to collude with, particularly if you are fed up with the image of the whimpering, useless woman, which is so often rammed down people's throats.

Women, quite simply, are equal. Not better or more skilful, not worse or less able—just equal. The image of physical strength is a dangerous one. Obviously the average man is physically stronger than the average woman, but a man who is physically weaker than another man does not expect to be assigned a lesser role in the workplace on this basis alone, so neither should a woman. Do not be drawn into the displays of prowess or ability which are often staged, consciously and subconsciously, by men in an attempt to impress female colleagues. It can sometimes appear to be harmless fun, but in reality the consequences can be very serious when the most able and physically developed male is called upon to sort out a problem concerning aggression and violence. It does no one any good at all.

RACISM

Overlapping the gender issues are those of race. Like the gender roles, there may have been a certain amount of change in society, but not nearly as much as is often presented to be the case. Racism can and does rear its ugly head, again and again, in the workplace. Whether attitudes are born of ignorance or bigotry or stupidity, the result is still the same—the isolating and stereotyping of other people on the basis of their perceived race or skin colour.

There is an unfortunate tendency in work settings to group together on the most simplistic basis. If a client or recipient of a service is, for example, of Asian origin, he or she is very likely to be assigned a worker who is perceived to be of the same racial origin. Other issues which one would expect to be taken into account, such as appropriateness on the basis of experience, viability or the actual contribution that particular worker can make, tend to be ignored. Thus if an individual who is Bengali comes to the office seeking help, she will most probably be given a Bengali worker, even if her specific problem is, for example, housing. The worker with housing expertise will be ignored. This pattern is repeated when it comes to aggression and violence. If someone of a certain ethnic origin is perceived as aggressive or violent, it is often assumed that a worker of the same racial group can alleviate the problem or sort it out. This, in my opinion and experience, is absolute nonsense: it does a great disservice to and puts a terrible degree of pressure on staff who are non-white or perceived as non-European.

23

It would be easy for me to say to people who find themselves in such situations, that they should resist or ignore that kind of treatment or should refuse to co-operate with it, but I know it is not that simple, any more than it is easy for people to break away from any predetermined role that others have set for them.

Changes are brought about little by little and step by step. The majority of white European people know next to nothing about the majority of non-white or non-European people who live in the same country. This is particularly true when considering the black community who may have parents of Afro-Caribbean origin. They know almost everything there is to know about white culture and white attitudes (particularly when it comes to black people), but how much do white people know about Afro-Caribbean culture?

Always remember, at work, just how little your white colleagues may actually know about you and be prepared, on issues of aggression and violence, to be put into situations not of your own making. They must be told, gently but firmly, how unfair and basically racist it is to suggest that you can solve a problem in relation to aggression and violence, simply because you appear to be of the same origin as the person displaying these traits.

All workers should make themselves aware, as far as possible, of the different cultural ways people have of expressing frustration and aggression. What may appear to be extremely aggressive to someone of one culture may, in another culture, simply be a way of making a point. Again, this cannot happen overnight. Time must be spent in learning, by listening to those who know, about some of the simple, taken-for-granted differences between people of different races and cultures.

If you are a white worker meeting for the first time someone whom you perceive as being extremely difficult or potentially violent, do not automatically assume, if you have a colleague of the same colour, that she will be able (or willing) to 'solve' the situation. There is no reason why you should not ask her for advice or guidance if she *appears* to share the same race or culture as your 'client', but you should not presume that she will be able to help you.

Nowhere are presumptions more dangerous and confusing than in the area of aggression and violence, particularly at work. At the end of the day, whether you feel comfortable with the reality or not, where race and culture are concerned, presumptions are racism in action! All they will do is isolate and disempower a fellow worker.

Finally, on this issue it is important to remember that if you are subjected to extreme aggression and/or physical violence by someone of a racial origin different from yours, you should not allow yourself to fall into the trap of thinking that the aggression is related to his race. You would then be likely to start feeling intimidated by and negative towards all other people of the same race, and then counselling or professional advice really ought to be considered. If you are white and a white person was violent towards you, you wouldn't say, 'He was violent because he is white, therefore I must avoid all white people,' so it follows that you should not allow yourself to think or say that about black people. If you do, however, try to avoid bottling it up: talk about it and get support where you can. If your work environment is unable to provide the kind of support or opportunity to talk through feelings which may be uncomfortable, there is a vast range of trained and accredited counsellors from whom you can seek advice independently.

THE NATURE OF AGGRESSION

One of the best things you can do, as workers, is get the issues of violence and aggression onto the agenda for discussion on a regular basis. I have worked in many different settings where this topic was covered—once! There seems to be a tendency to wait for someone to be beaten about or seriously abused before the problem is aired. Invariably the recipient of the aggression or violence is then off work or in hospital, like a traditional 'victim'. This is verging on the less than useless and promotes the unfortunate but under-standable atmosphere of 'I'm glad that wasn't me!' This basically helps no one as it just pushes the subject around rather than getting to grips with it.

Whilst understanding people's motives for verbal and physical violence can be helpful, this does not solve the immediate problem of not getting hit or hurt! Where the motivation of the person instigating the violence is linked to his or her individual situation, in which you have been involved as a worker, there are constraints and boundaries which are often mental as well as physical.

Many workers have been subjected to violence by people who are quite literally at the end of the line. They feel powerless, worthless and probably that they have lost everything they value. In some cases this may mean members of their family. Whilst this is understandable and more than worthy of considered analysis, it must still be accepted that people in these situa-tions can be very dangerous and potentially harmful to other human beings.

Let us look at the popular theories concerning violence and aggression. Abstract ideas may seem a little inadequate when a seventeen-stone scaffolder wants to cause you immediate and irreversible physical harm, but they are nevertheless a good place to start.

Instinct Theories

Based mainly on Freud's work, these theories have played a dominant role in people's thinking since the turn of the century. They are attractive and convenient as they argue that aggression is 'in' all of us and is therefore a natural instinct. Thus you have a relatively uncomplicated and straight-forward explanation of what is in fact a highly complex and sophisticated subject. The downside of these theories is that if they are true, then nothing can really be done to curb or control the aggressive instinct if it is so overwhelmingly 'natural' and a basic driving force motivating all mankind.

But there is also the question, unanswered, of exactly what an aggressive instinct is. Where is it? Why are some people more aggressive than others?

Whilst it is true that certain parts of the brain control physiological reactions in relation to aggression, they only actually switch on once we perceive a situation as a 'fight or flight' one. That perception is dictated by our previous learning. It is interesting to note that little effort is put into proving the existence of a natural 'flight' instinct, unlike that of the 'fight' instinct.

Frustration Theory

Due to the shortcomings of the instinct theories, frustration theory emerged in an attempt to address the imbalance. It basically argues that frustration is always a cause of aggression and that aggression is always a result of frustration.

This is an all-enveloping theory which fails to explain the fact that not all frustration leads to aggression. Some people just shrug it off or 'laugh' it off.

What is true is that when frustration is allied to personal attack, then aggression certainly has a part to play in the overall picture.

Social Learning Theory

This argument states that the concept of instincts and drives is a nonsense. It holds that aggression is learnt in a social context; thus aggressive behaviour is not innate but is learnt, and aggressive behaviour and feelings which are expressed are learnt by direct reward. The consequence of this, argue the social learning theorists, is that the majority of aggressive behaviour is learnt by copying behaviour witnessed in others, which is seen to result in positive reward. In other words, people who are aggressive seem to get what they want. Whilst this theory holds that the most effective types of people to copy are members of the same family or peer group, it also argues that there is such a thing as 'distance modelling' which is the copying of aggressive or violent behaviour seen on television, for example.

From this standpoint, aggression is more or less controlled by the human thought processes—what are known as 'cognitive' processes.

The advantage of this theory is that it examines real and actual behaviour in its context and attempts to explain it and to unravel those elements which lead up to it. Where it falls down is that it does not look at the whole person or his or her experiences, only at the circumstances of the violence or aggression. In addition, not enough attention is paid to the contributions of feelings or emotions and the part they play in the overall picture when attempting to understand and explain aggression and violence.

So what is aggression? It is in effect behaviour which is intended to produce damaging or hurtful effects on others, and this includes physical and emotional violence. It involves learnt habitual elements, and also fear when a situation appears to be out of control.

26

There are two main types of aggression—angry aggression and instrumental aggression.

Angry Aggression
By far the most common, this can be on a wide variety of levels. It involves emotional arousal, displacement (taking it out on others) and transference, where the aggression you are experiencing has been transferred from someone else.

Instrumental Aggression
A lot less common than the angry type, it is nevertheless very frightening. It is a cold, calculating attempt, seemingly without conscience, to gain maximum benefit for the perpetrator. The inhibitors such as empathy, guilt or anxiety appear to be suppressed or completely absent.

Whilst it is less common it still requires an ability to recognise it and to respond appropriately, and in the next section we shall examine those contributory factors which lead to aggression and violence and the conclusions we can draw from them.

FACTORS THAT TRIGGER AGGRESSION

Just why do people become aggressive or resort to violence? The theories we have just looked at certainly describe the different types of aggression and make the link from frustration to aggression to violence, but the simple fact is that every individual is different.

You know yourself that, on one day, something like sitting in a car in a traffic jam might not upset you at all, while on another day, under a different set of circumstances, you feel extremely agitated, possibly aggressive and, if a situation developed further, potentially violent—yet it is the same traffic jam, the only thing that is different is you. What may have changed is how you perceive your situation and how damaging you consider it to be stuck in that traffic jam: your perceptions and emotions have altered.

This is true for everyone. What is not commonly understood is that the change is not always immediately visible or obvious, but it can take just one little thing to spark it off. After that it is up to the individual's natural or enforced inhibitors. An enforced inhibitor can be the perceived perception of the consequences of being violent. In other words, you have visualised the consequences of your actions and the effect they may have on you or others around you. For example, you may think to yourself, 'I would like to get out of my car and jump up and down on the bonnet of the car in front because that driver pulled out in front of me!' But the reality is that the driver might punch you, or call the police and have you charged with criminal damage, and then you would find that a criminal conviction was not compatible with your employment, so you would lose your job. If you lost your job there would be

27

more pressure on your family life. Your marriage might crumble and your wife walk out, taking the children with her. So it goes on in your mind in a type of pattern. You go through each step and its consequence, and you basically see that the consequence of your aggression or possible violence simply isn't worth it.

Of course, not everyone thinks like this or is governed by the same conditions. If you haven't got a job, then you are not going to worry about losing it. If you have no prospects of getting a job, then you are not going to be overly concerned about the effect a criminal conviction might have on your chances of being offered one. Likewise, if you haven't got a family or children, you are not going to think about the effect of your actions upon them. This is not to say that all unemployed, unmarried, childless males are prone to violence—far from it—just that there can be circumstantial situations that govern individuals' courses of action when it comes to aggression and violence.

Many of the people who come into contact with services such as health, social services, police, community advice and so on, are likely to be under severe pressure, even if it is only short-term. This is an important point to remember when making the mistake of putting people into pre-set categories.

A homeless, unsupported person who has spent a lifetime of dealing with welfare services may well be less prone to frustration, aggression and physical violence than a fully-employed member of the professional classes who has never had to deal with support services before. He may consider it an admission of failure that he is in contact with your office at all, and could already be harbouring a smouldering resentment which is covered up by the social niceties which he has spent a lifetime honing to perfection. The aggression could come without any warning, and often does.

So what actually happens when people become violent, and what effect can fear have on individuals? It is all a question of degree in that everyone's physical make-up differs.

PHYSICAL EFFECTS OF AGGRESSION AND FEAR

Generally speaking, when someone becomes aggressive and violent he experiences a dramatically increased blood flow, and if he is feeling angry rather than scared he will be in a state of hyperactivity and at a physical peak. This means that things which might ordinarily have an effect on him may have no effect at all. This is important to consider, particularly if he is someone you are used to dealing with. Speaking to him in a certain way or threatening him with a certain course of action (if you both live in an institution) may have the opposite effect on him: instead of calming him, it will make him worse. Be prepared to find that something you try does not work. It is no use giving up at the first hurdle, and by giving up I do not mean walking (or running) away, as this may actually be the most appropriate way to handle the situation. Giving up means just standing there, unwilling to consider any other course of action, in the vain hope that he will just stop. He could also be experiencing great anger, possibly quite unconnected with you, and again this may have a dramatic effect on his physical capacities.

Increased anger can result in an increase in physical strength. Or that is how it appears. What has happened is that the anger has subdued the body's natural physical inhibitors. Fear can also have the same effect.

The speed at which someone can move is dictated by his or her muscle power. When there is an increase in body heat (as a result of anger or stress), this has a direct effect on the muscles. It only takes a rise of two degrees in body heat to result in an increase of up to 20 per cent in muscular action. Thus someone who is being aggressive or potentially violent towards you may be able to move a lot quicker than you realise.

In everyday living you use your body, breathing, walking, running and so on. The demands you make directly affect your heart and lungs. This is basically what is meant by 'circulo-respiratory capacity', and is what is worked on when you do exercise classes such as the popular aerobics at fitness centres.

The capacity of your circulo-respiratory system dictates how much physical activity you can do at any given time. When you find that you can only keep going for short periods, it is not actually about muscle strength but about how much breath you have and what is happening to your heart. This is what controls your physical level. But when you are under a physical threat, various reactions take place.

The famous expression is 'fight or flight', which simply means the reaction to stressful situations. There is a cluster of nerve-cells in the brain, the hypothalamus, which governs the involuntary reactions of the body and in turn has an effect on the pituitary gland which releases hormones into the blood supply.

The result, on the human body, is tension in the muscles, a quickening of breath, an increase in the heart rate and a rise in blood pressure. There is also a reaction in the spleen which causes an increase in the red corpuscles that carry oxygen, necessary to support physical activity, and an increase of oxygen to the brain and heart, resulting in a greater amount of available energy. At the same time your throat tightens, which in turns restricts your breathing, despite the increased availability of oxygen.

As well as all the above, if you are injured you will lose less blood than usual, because the surface blood vessels shrink. The bowels and bladder also loosen dramatically, often resulting in a complete loss of muscular control in that region of your body. Some people are rooted to the spot, paralysed with absolute fear, but the physical reactions carry on regardless, which is why so many people feel strange after such an event—'as though I was watching a film of someone else' is a common statement from people who have been the targets of someone else's extreme aggression or violence.

One of the most useful things you can do in situations which bring about the physical reactions I have just described is to make a real effort to concentrate, not so much on what is going on around you as on your breathing. Rather than just breathing in air to your chest, which will be feeling very tight anyway, try to bring the air, in a steady and even way, down to the diaphragm, the area just around the belly button.

This has the effect of dramatically increasing your control over your breathing and reducing the debilitating effect of the fear on your physical capacities, thus allowing you to take some course of physical action to ensure your well-being, such as running away or defending yourself, although my definition of defending yourself actually includes running away—it is one of the best forms of self-defence known to human kind and has been used since time began. You are doing nothing wrong by walking away!

At the same time as trying to control your breathing, resist the temptation to draw yourself up to your full height, rather you should lower your centre of gravity, as though the very breath you are drawing in is flowing all around your body. This has the physical benefit of helping the supply of oxygen, and the emotional benefit of actually giving you back a feeling of control and internal power.

It is one thing to theorise about aggression and violence, and another actually to face it. The mixture of emotions that it unleashes in the individual can surprise, frighten and disturb, all at the same time. Hardly anyone can deny that there is at least one situation, which they may already have experienced, the very thought of which fills them with naked fear, and in the aftermath their minds will be buzzing with questions: 'Why does it happen?' 'When does it happen?' 'What should I do about it?' 'Was it my fault?' 'What should I have done differently?'

There are no simple and convenient answers, but what can be learnt is the control and management of aggression and of physical and verbal violence and abuse.

2 Colour Coding

Whenever you are dealing with another human being who may be under some kind of stress, there is always a chance that you might be subjected to verbal abuse, aggression or physical violence.

It is crucial that your response should be the most appropriate for you and the man or woman confronting you, and you must remember that your physical and emotional well-being should not be sacrificed just because you are scared of injuring, hurting, or simply offending the other person.

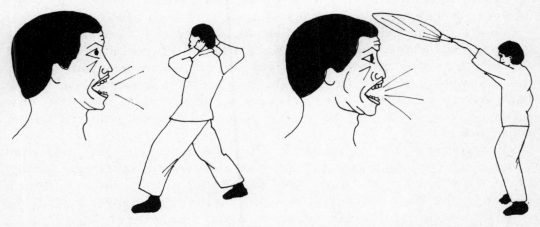

If someone uses offensive language or shouts at you in a bullying and unpleasant way, obviously it is overreacting to beat him with a stick. By the same token, if he has you pinned against the wall, with his hands round your throat, you will have to consider a wider and more physically demanding range of options, rather than just hoping that he will calm down!

The great weakness of advice given in many publications on the subject of self-defence is that it does not take into account the personalities and psychological make-up of the people it expects to perform a given technique in the interests of self-preservation. For example, you may be advised to 'jab your fingers in your aggressor's eyes' in response to a physical attack. But the simple truth is that the vast majority of people would have great difficulty in bringing themselves to do something like that, simply because it is alien to their personality or attitude to life. Even if you could reconcile yourself to performing such an aggressive and dangerous action, your chances of doing it successfully would actually be quite slim, unless you had practised it!

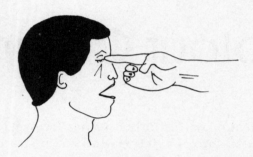

It follows, then, that such advice is pretty useless if you are physically and emotionally incapable of the level of aggression required to carry it out. When we are under enormous pressure and are convinced that our lives are in danger, we can and often do surprise ourselves by what we are prepared to do in order to survive. But the reality is that, all too often, the attack happens and is all over before we even realise that we were in danger.

Using a colour code is a great help in working out a response that is appropriate and realistic for you. Make a list of all the different types of aggression and violence that you might face in the course of your work or daily life, even if they have never happened, place them in order, starting with the mildest, and attach a colour to each category; then work out what measures you would find acceptable to protect yourself, your friends or colleagues.

The different colours relate to the seriousness of the individual experiences. Obviously, being screamed at can be very upsetting emotionally, but it is clearly not in the same category as being attacked with a knife or a broken bottle. The colours also distinguish between the danger levels of the experiences: no one ever suffered serious injury from being shouted at, but a knife attack can be fatal.

Let us look at a possible colour coding for the different experiences:

GREEN = uncomfortable
YELLOW = threatening
BLUE = physical attack
RED = serious injury or death

It is possible that you yourself find it difficult to associate the colour red with serious injury or death. If that is so, then just rearrange the colours until they are in an order or pattern which you can relate to. Let us look at the categories one by one.

GREEN: UNCOMFORTABLE

This covers a wide range of actions, suggestions or attitudes that you personally find uncomfortable, such as verbal abuse involving racial or sexual harassment, or simply someone shouting at you for no apparent reason. This is often the case if you are a 'front-line' worker such as a duty nurse, duty social worker or similar, working in direct contact with the public from whom you are not separated by a plexiglass screen.

Green is a very important stage: you may choose to react in a non-assertive way, which may have the desired outcome, or the situation may escalate into the next stages, since an individual may become more and more aggressive if unchallenged. It is all down to personal choice, but you must know what choices are open to you.

CATEGORY	POSSIBLE REASONS	POSSIBLE CHOICES
Green	Silence or threatening manner	Enquire what is wrong
	Invasion of personal space	
	Offensive remarks or suggestions	Ask him or her to stop
	Refusal to acknowledge you	Mirror back (do the same to them)
	Aggressive physical presentation	
	Shouting or screaming	Cover your ears
	Overpowering body odour	Leave the room
	Breaking wind	Do nothing
		Get a colleague to join you

The circumstances vary from setting to setting. What you must do is decide, depending on the nature of your job and your place of work, what you will and will not accept. Some settings will always be uncomfortable—they go with the job—but that does not mean that you have to be at unreasonable risk of physical assault.

There is a confusion amongst people who work in direct contact with the public about the difference between acceptable and unacceptable behaviour, but until that is sorted out you, the face-to-face worker, have to take responsibility for your own and your colleagues' well-being.

Under the Green category I have listed a number of possible reasons why you might feel less than comfortable, due to someone else's behaviour. Before deciding that the person is deliberately trying to intimidate you, it is worth considering certain factors that you should take into account:

Silence or threatening manner
Can he speak the same language as you? Does he have a learning difficulty? Does he have a speech impediment? Is he hearing impaired?

Invasion of personal space
Does he possess different cultural values from yours?

Offensive remarks or suggestions
Does he know he is being offensive?

Refusal to acknowledge you
Can he see you? Does he know who you are?

Aggressive physical presentation
Does he know he is being aggressive? Is it a gender issue? Is he more aggressive to one sex than to another?

Shouting or screaming
Some people do not know they are talking or shouting loudly until they are informed of the fact.

Overpowering body odour
Could be due to a medical condition, hot weather, or even a specific type of deodorant (there is a type manufactured in the United States which is specifically designed to resemble male body odour!).

Breaking wind
Could be a medical condition. You should also be aware that some cultures do not consider this offensive, even if it is done in public.

These are just a few of the possible explanations. If none of them seems to justify what is happening, then it is highly probable that you are being subjected to some kind of abuse. Sometimes people will use threats to get what they want.

If we look in greater detail at the reasons for your discomfort, we can see that a lot depends on your ability to communicate. There is a convention in many professional settings which supports the notion that you must not let someone know that you are afraid, as that will just make him worse or feel insecure. I don't know where this idea comes from and I have not seen any powerful evidence to support it. If someone is frightening you by being silent then, in my opinion, the best thing you can do is tell him. If he does not mean to frighten you, he will address the situation immediately; if, however, his intention is to intimidate you and he has succeeded, you might as well let him know and save yourself a lot of extended abuse or pressure. At this stage I think there is nothing wrong in leaving the room, so that the interview can take place on another day. Obviously, if the person has suffered a loss or is under great pressure, the circumstances may be different, but if that is the case then often the intention was not to scare you—in fact you may be the last thing on his mind. It is just a matter of ascertaining the facts, then making the most appropriate decision.

There is nothing wrong in asking someone to stop behaviour which you find upsetting or threatening. Again, if the person understands what you are asking but refuses to stop, there is a further range of options for you to consider, such as terminating the discussion or refusing to be drawn farther into the proceedings until the source of your distress or discomfort is addressed.

This is a crucial point. The comfort and well-being of the person you are trying to help is very important, but so is yours! You must not allow yourself to be dragged into a situation in which his comfort and sense of being in control are gained at great expense to yourself. You are unlikely to be of much use to him, in a professional sense, if you are continually subjected to unnecessary discomfort or abuse.

One of the possible choices I listed was mirroring back—basically doing to him what he is doing to you. This has to be considered very carefully and I suggest that you do not attempt it without the backing and support of your immediate supervisor. It can be a very useful way of modifying someone's behaviour, particularly of an unacceptable type, if it is part of a planned work programme. But if it is just an instant reaction to a given situation, it requires a high degree of poise, self-assurance and strength of purpose to bring it to a successful conclusion, rather than causing an escalation of a difficult situation. It can be particularly useful in working with adolescents.

If you are subjected to offensive remarks, particularly of a sexual nature, don't just sit there and take it: there is no reason why you should have to be subjected to it. Sitting there and hoping he will stop is not the answer. You have to let him know that he is putting himself in the wrong by what he is saying. You are not in the wrong for being who or what you are. It goes without saying that the same applies to racist remarks, which are never warranted and, in my opinion, cannot be justified in any circumstances, whoever makes them.

I was told by a worker in a social security office that one of her worst memories was of a man who was not getting what he wanted. He stripped naked in the public foyer, then, when no action seemed to be forthcoming to meet his demands, he threatened to masturbate in public. The police arrived before he commenced the threatened deed.

This may seem humorous, but the reality is that the closer you are to such incidents, the less funny they become; they are examples, of the rawest kind, of vulnerable human beings being prepared to go to extraordinary lengths to get what they feel is the appropriate response to their problem.

So let us assume that you are faced with behaviour which you would place in the Green category. This allows you to explore the options in a centred and focused way and to look at the possibility that there might be a misunderstanding in the communication process. If someone is deliberately trying to offend or threaten you, it is best to find that out as quickly as possible, so that you can make an appropriate decision with greater clarity and precision.

Verbal Assault

Violence in the work setting is not just the highly serious physical assaults which have a detrimental effect on employees who are subjected to them. Verbal assault is equally distressing and can often have a long-term effect on those who are exposed to it. Sarah, a nurse in a busy central London hospital, certainly feels this way: 'I actually find the verbal stuff more upsetting than the physical assaults. At least the bruises heal, but I've never been able to take being shouted at or screamed at—I don't know why—I just don't! Outwardly I appear calm and collected but inside I just go to pieces. The trouble is that I don't know who to turn to as the general feeling seems to be, better to be shouted at than punched! But for me that just isn't true!'

Under the Health and Safety at Work Act 1974 (HSW Act), employers must provide for the health and safety of their employees, and this covers employees who face a predictable risk of violence, which nurses clearly do in the course of their everyday duties.

After the death of a social worker in 1986, the DHSS set up a Committee on Violence, headed by Lord Skelmersdale. Their conclusion was that 'where violent incidents are foreseeable employers have a duty, under Section 2 of the Act, to identify the nature and extent of the risk and to devise measures which provide a safe workplace and a safe system of work'. Clearly, if verbal assaults make an employee feel unsafe or ill at ease in her place of work, then there is a responsibility on the part of the employer to ensure that something is done to alleviate this.

In the nursing, social work and transport services, one of the reasons why this does not seem to happen is because, in my opinion, employers do not take verbal assault seriously. The employee who appears unable to take this kind of 'pressure' is identified as possibly being unsuitable for his or her job. This clearly is very unfair.

In police work the situation is rather different, since abusing an officer verbally is an arrestable offence; at the very least, the employee (the policeman or woman) can actually do something about it. At the same time, however, one must not underestimate the effect, over a period of time, that continued verbal abuse can have on an individual's nerves and confidence in the execution of his or her duties.

If you are simply unprepared to put up with verbal assault (and I suggest that this is the correct approach, whatever your area of work), then you really do need the support, sympathy and understanding of your manager. If the person immediately above you in the chain of command is unsympathetic, it is very difficult to make a stand about what you will and will not tolerate. It is a good idea to get this sorted out before you find yourself in a situation where you need support. If you know that he or she is unsympathetic, you are in a better position, forewarned, than if you only discover it when you are feeling isolated, vulnerable or exposed.

It is worth being clear about definitions and making sure that your employer also understands what is meant by violence. The Health and Safety Executive's (HSE) booklet 'Violence to Staff' sees violence as 'any incidence in which an employee is abused, threatened or assaulted by a member of the public in circumstances arising out of the course of his or her employment' (NALGO—Violence at Work Paper, July 1992). It often comes as a shock to employers to find out that verbal assault is actually accepted as violence by national bodies in the way that it is.

It is difficult to lay down general rules about how you should react to verbal assault because what is possible in one profession may be impossible in another. If you are a police officer involved in the execution of your duties, you cannot respond in the same way as, say, a social worker who has made a conscious decision not to tolerate a particular type of behaviour.

A police officer cannot simply walk away, leave the room or 'mirror back' a certain type of attitude or behaviour from a member of the public, his or her range of choices is therefore different from those of a social worker, although some social workers may argue that their options are exactly the same. I would disagree with this view: there are times and situations when leaving a room or treating a client in the same offensive way he treats you may be appropriate for a social worker. The same cannot be said for the police.

There are, however, structures and boundaries affecting the role of the police, which can be to their advantage. If, in the eyes of the law, there appears to be no need for an interview to continue, or for an officer to remain in the presence of a member of the public, then he or she can indeed simply terminate the interview or encounter and go about his or her business. The law thus acts as a type of support.

This is not so clear-cut in social work where it is really a matter of individual interpretation. The social worker can justify her action or explain it after the event, but she does not have the convenience of legislation to support her.

In the field of nursing and health care there are equally difficult areas. An individual who is being verbally abusive may, in the opinion of the health worker, require medical assistance. If this is the case then it is impossible for her to walk away and be able to justify it afterwards, particularly if physical assault does not appear to be the issue. It is a complicated situation. From a purely personal point of view, I feel that no one should have to be subjected to any kind of abuse and that a health worker should be entitled to walk away from someone who is abusing her, but then I'm not in her situation. I am not the one who would have to explain and justify the action afterwards to sometimes unsympathetic supervisors.

Whether an action is appropriate or inappropriate is a very important point, particularly in the health care setting, and should not be confused with right and wrong as it so often is. It is very easy for a supervisor, after the event, to say that you should not have walked away but should have stayed to provide care or medical assistance irrespective of any threatened or actual verbal assault. Do not get involved in the argument about right and wrong:

the issue is appropriate and inappropriate responses. It may very well be wrong to walk away from someone who is acknowledged to be a patient or client, but at the same time, if your exposure to abuse or assault is making it impossible for you to deliver the correct level of care, then you have to consider the other patients or clients who could be benefiting from your time and attention.

Far too often, in the social work, health care, police and transport services, the issues are debated after the event by supervisors who, quite simply, were not there at the time and therefore could not 'taste' the environment or the atmosphere, or judge what was appropriate or inappropriate behaviour.

This, in my opinion, is quite wrong. By the time the occurrence is being considered by other professionals (your supervisor and superiors in the workplace), the situation will have changed completely. The individual known as the 'patient' or 'client' will no longer be there and several days will probably have passed. The inquiry may not even be held in the same building or the same town.

The reality is that if the supervisor was making a judgement about your response or course of action with the client or patient screaming down his neck and making the same threats, the chances are that he would take a quite different view.

Make no mistake about it, then: verbal assault is violence. What varies is the professional setting and the extent to which you can respond to it, while safeguarding your own well-being and making sure that your motives and responses will not be misunderstood afterwards.

At the end of the day, you are being paid by the taxpayer to do a job. You have a responsibility, both to yourself and to the general public, to ensure that you are able to complete your duties to the best of your ability. You cannot do this at the same time as being verbally or physically assaulted.

There may be times when walking away is simply not an option. Many people say that they have experienced satisfactory results (they were not attacked!) by a variety of methods. One is to keep your voice low, not allowing it to rise above a certain level, in order to convey a feeling of non-aggression towards the other person. Another is to make yourself physically lower than the other person, such as sitting on the floor or not standing up, even if he is towering above you, possibly shouting at you or waving his finger in your face. It may be tempting to leap to your feet when someone is physically above you, but there are times when it is advisable to keep yourself lower and 'smaller' so that he does not see you as a threat.

Another method is simply to say nothing at all. Just sit there with an impassive face, saying and doing nothing, and the storm will pass. Obviously you would need to have a fair degree of self-control and inner confidence before you tried that way of resolving a situation.

Whichever way you choose to play it, assuming that you are not frightened out of your wits and can still think clearly, remember that it is your decision—you are the person at whom the abuse is being directed, for whatever reason; you are the victim, and that gives you the right to make a choice to protect your well-being.

YELLOW: THREATENING

It is reasonable to assume that at this stage there is less room for confusion. If you feel extremely threatened you would be wise to take action, and the likelihood of any confusion due to different cultural perceptions is somewhat less.

CATEGORY	POSSIBLE REASONS	POSSIBLE CHOICES
Yellow	You are pinned against a wall	Resist and struggle
	Spat at	Return the same
	Person makes a gesture to strike	Lie on the floor
	You are pushed and shoved	Leave the room
	Grabbed, held and shouted at	Cry
	Told what you can and cannot do, i.e. do not leave the room, do not pick up the phone	Do what you are told
	You are blamed specifically for the individual's life problems	Agree/disagree/refuse to listen
	You are told he has a weapon	Pretend lack of interest
	He tells you he may hurt or kill you	Ask why/don't ask why
		Pretend to have a panic attack
		Actually have a panic attack
		Hit the emergency button (if there is one)

If at all possible, on of the best courses of action when you feel really uncomfortable or isolated is to remove yourself from the situation. If this is difficult to do, make an excuse to explain why you must leave the room, but only be less than truthful if you really feel that by being honest about your degree of discomfort you might inflame the situation and make your aggressor more intimidating. Otherwise it really is worthwhile letting him know that you are uncomfortable or even afraid, and that you would prefer the interview or meeting to continue at another time or place, even with someone else present.

I know that things are not always that simple, but it is worth thinking along these lines, whether the situation involves people for whom you are providing a service, or even whether your aggressor is someone with whom you work. Racism and sexual harassment, whilst not being strictly in the category of physical violence, still have the same effect on the people who are subjected to them. If the aggression happens in a work setting they feel uncomfortable, threatened, intimidated, insecure, angry, unsure what to do.

In all the above situations one thing is certain: it is not your fault. People must learn that they cannot get away with that kind of behaviour. One of the first steps to learning is to comprehend that they are in the wrong, not you!

I know some people suggest that a good way to combat this type of situation is to use humour, but I am not so sure. There is actually nothing funny about it, and people tend not to realise how frightened you are if you are cracking jokes in an attempt to soothe the situation. It is very common for some individuals to be surprised at how upsetting their behaviour is to other people, once it is pointed out to them.

Of course there are also those who couldn't care less. Their sole purpose is to harass sexually, racially or physically, and that is when some of the choices in the Yellow category come into play. Another extremely effective option, in which no one gets hurt, is to scream very loudly. This has the effect of surprise, giving you enough time to remove yourself from the scene.

If you can get the opportunity, always tell your supervisor at once of any incident which has arisen and explain your behaviour clearly and concisely. Remember the important difference between right, wrong, appropriate and inappropriate. You may have taken a course of action which your boss or supervisor subsequently feels was wrong, such as screaming at a client, but you must hold on to the fact that you felt what you did was appropriate under the circumstances rather than 'right'. The issue is about choice in a given situation, rather than about who is right or who is wrong.

Perhaps you have been able to identify certain signs that suggest people are under stress and likely to take it out on you. This is not always the case—sometimes people can turn on you without any warning—but bearing that in mind, there are times when you can detect certain elements appearing, which represent tension in the person confronting you.

Your tone of voice, self-control and degree of concentration can all play a part in bringing about a successful conclusion to such a situation. It is worth looking out for these signs, if only because real violence or extreme aggression can have the effect of completely freezing you to the spot, and you want to avoid that if at all possible.

Certain parts of the human body are quite useful indicators of how someone is feeling. Watch the hands and see how they are being used to make a point—perhaps an action such as cutting the air, or a clenched fist in a punching motion.

If the arms are crossed this is usually a sign that all is not well, but if the arms are open the person may be a little more relaxed. You should be aware of these signs in yourself, too. If your arms are uncrossed and you avoid using clenched fists or sudden swiping movements with your hands, or sudden movements away from your client or towards him, you can help to create a calm and relaxed atmosphere.

As with the Green category, under Yellow your options will differ according to your type of employment. A police officer can arrest someone who starts to display some of the behaviour described above. This is not possible in other professions, and likewise some of the alternative responses are just not an option in all professional settings.

In an office dealing with people who are recipients of a social work service, it may be appropriate to lie on the floor, with the aim of appearing non-aggressive, but if you are driving the number 36 bus, late at night, to Peckham in South London, this is not possible. However, there are other ways, often involving unusual or strange responses, which can help a situation.

I was actually on a number 36 bus to Peckham when an individual, clearly irate and disturbed, got on the bus and insisted on paying his fare with a ginger biscuit, which he carefully took out of the packet. When the bus conductor just looked at the biscuit in his hand, the man said, 'You're quite right, the fare's more than that,' and he duly took out another biscuit and placed it in the conductor's hand. The conductor looked at the biscuits for a moment, then broke a piece off one of them and handed it back to the man. 'There's your change—it's only one and a half to Peckham!' He then moved on up the bus and collected the rest of the fares.

The man took the half biscuit, put it back in his packet and said, 'Thank you, when did the fares go down?' The conductor replied with absolutely no trace of humour in his voice, 'Last week—they thought two biscuits were too much!'

The man sat quietly until the bus reached his stop. As he got off he turned to the conductor and said, 'Thanks, mate—if only everyone was as honest as you!' Everyone on the bus, including the conductor, heaved a sigh of relief.

Now technically the bus conductor should have collected the correct legal tender from everyone on his bus, but he took a course of action which he considered appropriate under the circumstances and which ensured his well-being and the well-being of the other passengers on the bus. We have no way of knowing what would have happened if he had insisted on money for the fare, but the chances are it would have turned nasty.

Assaults on staff on public transport are unfortunately very common. Various countermeasures are available and employers have resorted to them—for example, London Buses' 4,100 driver only buses are fitted with special driver protection screens. There are also video camera facilities and staff undergo training programmes to help them deal with violence.

However, all that security is useless unless understanding is there as well.

41

If the conductor on the number 36 had found himself in trouble for taking the action he did, then his confidence to respond in subsequent situations would have been quite seriously diminished.

Clearly, certain situations can escalate into more physical confrontations if they are not handled in a particular way. In practice staff such as bus or tube workers, police officers and health workers are often working in the dark, meeting a member of the public for the first time. Social workers are more likely to come into contact with people whom they see more than once, unless they are part of the 'duty' system', whereby they meet people, often for the first time, to attempt to deal with their problems.

This is always in an office setting, and it may be helpful to consider some of the options listed in the Yellow category. Again, it is important to remember the consequences of your actions and to keep a grasp of your aim, which is to ensure your well-being, not to be smart or a solver of every conceivable problem.

Some of the responses outlined on p. 39 may actually come naturally. For example, you may cry in certain situations out of pure fear rather than a calculated effort to defuse the situation, but the response may be the same. People sometimes do not know how upsetting their behaviour is, particularly if they make a habit of behaving like that and no one ever tells them or is too scared—understandably so—actually to challenge them.

Some offices have an emergency or 'panic' button, but there is no point in having one unless individuals are around to respond. In other words, what do you do when you hear the panic button?

I worked in one office where the panic button was not linked to anywhere! It just make a loud noise and no one had ever agreed what should be done if they actually heard the alarm being sounded. They just lived in hope that it wouldn't happen to them—that they wouldn't be around on the day someone actually pressed the button.

The Yellow category highlights the need for planning and co-ordination in relation to violence and aggression. It is impossible to predict how an individual may react in a given situation, but organisations and departments can develop a strategy and simple step-by-step responses to situations which threaten their staff.

Unfortunately a lot of groups and individuals think that guidelines are enough. They aren't! Guidelines do not provide the kind of support which encourages people to take the appropriate course of action when they are under threat. Guidelines do not constitute an agreement between the face-to-face workers about what should happen when one of them is assaulted. This is an important point. Guidelines only suggest how things should be and ideally what should happen in a given situation; they are not accurate representations of what actually happens.

If violence and aggression are discussed amongst staff, then a common understanding can be built up about what is considered threatening and

42

unacceptable. This is crucial, as opinions vary. In a staff group setting, or any situation involving employees, it is vital to have agreement about the lowest common denominator with regard to threatening behaviour, so that there is no confusion about when to support fellow staff members and when not to intervene.

Individual employers have a responsibility, not often met, to ensure that if someone has a history of violence, then members of staff coming into contact with that individual are informed as of right. If nothing else, the terms and conditions of health and safety at work demand it. If an employer knowingly puts you in a situation which is potentially hazardous to your health, then he has failed in his duty to ensure and promote your well-being.

This may appear over-precise, but it is important: information pertinent and relevant to your job, and the correct level of support, demand openness and honesty about the people and situations you may be dealing with. I know that sometimes the reasons for not being open about someone's aggressive or violent tendencies may stem from a well-meaning attempt to avoid distressing a worker, or worrying her. But the reality is that we all have a right to information which affects us, thus enabling us to make professional and informed decisions about a given situation.

BLUE: PHYSICAL ATTACK

Wherever possible, situations involving physical contact should be avoided, but sometimes the matter is not in your hands—the aggressor has made the decision to attempt to control or hurt you physically. How you respond is obviously a question of degree. If you are a carer in a home for elderly people and an old lady grabs your hair and will not let go, you do not punch her in the face—quite clearly that would be unacceptable, presuming that all she is doing is pulling your hair and no weapon is involved. At the end of the day, however, you cannot just stand there while your hair is pulled and your head tugged back and forth. Alternatively, your hands may be grabbed by someone who should not be holding you and you wish to break free without causing injury. In both cases there are options open to you which we shall be looking at in later chapters.

Types of Physical Attack in the Blue Category

You may be faced with any of the following siutations from which you must try to extricate yourself without seriously injuring your aggressor:

A grab on one or both wrists
A grab around the throat
Being held from the rear or around the neck
Someone on top of you with you on the ground
Being held from the rear whilst you are in a seated position
Hair-pulling from the front or from behind

Before looking at possible responses it is worth considering certain zones around the human body. The public zone would be a distance of about 10–25 feet. This is the kind of distance which would be between you and other people in a public setting. The social zone would be about five to ten feet depending on the circumstances. The personal zone can be seen in terms of two to five feet and would be the kind of distance you would expect between two people having a conversation with each other. The intimate zone is one of privacy and you would not expect someone to be in that zone without your permission; he or she would usually be a family member or a close friend.

These zones are important as they allow us to qualify certain situations and provide us with a degree of flexibility if we are unsure about what is happening. If someone moves from one zone to another uninvited, you simply move away. If he continues to invade your space, the chances are that you have a problem on your hands which you can resolve in one of many ways, possibly by using one of the responses already discussed under the Green and Yellow categories.

An important point to remember is that unless someone is threatening to throw something at you or shoot you, you are safe if he is in the public or social zones; it is only when he moves into the other zones that you are at risk of physical attack. You can therefore gauge the situation and think about what you are going to do or not do, assuming that you have time. Sometimes violence strikes without warning, and then things do get physical. In subsequent chapters we shall be considering what to do in the course of such unfortunate but all too frequent events.

If you have the opportunity, I always say run away and keep yourself in one piece. If the violence has started, forget about trying to preserve the situation and think about preserving yourself! This is very important as often vital seconds can be lost in trying to sort out a situation which has already left your control.

I attended a training course once, on violence. A video film was shown featuring a large, shaven-headed, tattooed man smashing up an office, throwing the desks, books and files around before breaking the windows, ripping off his shirt and howling like a wolf. He turned to the camera, pointed a finger and, screwing up his face, snarled, 'Right—you're next!' The film then went dead. Everyone in the group was asked what they would do next, and how they would best resolve the situation.

There was a variety of well-meaning and carefully thought-out responses, but I must be honest and admit that I said that if the angry man was kind enough to inform me that I was next and there was a door available which he was not blocking, then I was off! I wasn't going to hang around to be physically injured.

Before going further we need to look at the Red category because it can be the outcome of some of the physical attacks in the Blue category if they are not dealt with successfully.

RED: SERIOUS INJURY OR DEATH

Attacks with weapons are not uncommon on staff in a wide variety of settings. As well as the obvious knives or heavy metal objects, everyday articles such as ashtrays may also be used as weapons, or chairs which are not secured to the ground.

I have known instances when social services staff have actually been shot in the course of their duties, or when someone has hired another individual to commit a serious assault on a social worker. The same thing also happens in the other professions.

Red Category Attacks

The following all have the potential to result in serious injury or death:

Attacks to your throat, head or vulnerable parts of your body.

Throttling round your throat or neck.

Threats or actual attack with a weapon such as a chair, broken bottle, piece of office equipment or knife.

My advice is never to try to defend yourself against a weapon. Everything happens so fast that it is all over before you even realise it. You must do everything in your power to remove yourself from the situation as fast as possible, avoiding the notion of being some kind of negotiator. Don't hang around to prove a point if there is somewhere to run; you may well live to regret it—or not as the case may be. Generally there is little warning before someone attempts to use a weapon on you. If there is a warning, then that is when you must be planning your escape.

When this rule may not apply is when other innocent people are involved, possibly other individuals who are recipients of a service. You may not be able to bring yourself just to run away and leave them to it, although if you did I, for one, would not blame you: it is a natural human reaction to run away. However, if you feel that you must stay to protect someone else or a group of other people, you should try to work out in your mind exactly what you hope to achieve and how.

It is no use staying around unless you can contribute something to alleviate the situation, presuming that you have time to think about it. Sometimes people are hailed as heroes because they did not run away but stayed to help other vulnerable victims, but the reality may be that they just didn't have a chance to get away! No disgrace, just a fact which is often ignored after an event.

The ignoring of facts is a very common practice, particularly when dealing with organisations which you may be working for. Make a note of everything that happened, leading up to an incident, during an incident and after it, making sure that you highlight the minor and major players in the situation and what they contributed to the outcome. You must be absolutely clear about this. If another individual is injured or killed as a result of your actions, and the incident happens in the course of your work, time is not on your side when it comes to ensuring that everyone who matters is in possession of the full facts.

It is far easier for an organisation, and this applies equally to transport staff, social workers, police, nurses and so on, to suggest that a member of staff or a group of staff acted inappropriately or made the wrong individual decision or series of decisions, than to admit that there was no guidance or support from the organisation itself. You must be aware of this, regardless of your position. It is foolish to think that all outcomes are governed by the truth and a sense of fair play. Reality is just not like that. Self-interest and preservation of the organisation will always take precedence over admitting that systems or styles of management should change.

Let us look at some of the physical realities of situations in the Blue and Red categories.

If someone is choking you and will not let go, the brain may be starved of oxygen and brain damage may occur, or even death. Likewise, if someone is on top of you with his hands round your throat, death can easily result—not to mention the possibility that it may be a sexually motivated assault.

So what should you do? In practice, physical responses are only an appropriate course of action when you are attempting to defend yourself. They are not an option when you merely feel distressed or uneasy about a situation. If someone physically attacks you, you have a right to look after yourself.

In so doing, however, it is important to remember the law in relation to self-defence. Section three of the Criminal Law Act 1967 relates to that famous phrase 'use of reasonable force' in the act of defending yourself. If, having escaped from someone's clutches, you proceed to jump up and down on his head, when clearly he was going to be of no further danger to you, then you have exceeded the boundaries of what is known as 'reasonable force'.

Similarly, if you are attacked by someone with a weapon, it is not self-defence to take it from him and then use it against him, even though at the time this may seem perfectly reasonable. Your employers and a court of law will probably take a very dim view, unless of course you are able to prove that you panicked or that the weapon was used accidentally in the course of a struggle.

At the end of the day it comes down to individual interpretation; there will always be an element of risk in any kind of response, whatever it may be.

The step-by-step process of putting things into categories can help you to think more clearly in times of stress, so that you need not waste time worrying about outcome, consequences or circumstances when you should be concentrating on your own physical well-being.

If you think the situation is a Green one, then you are obviously going to be more relaxed than if it is Yellow, Blue or Red. The colour can automatically instil in you a sense of urgency, immediacy and danger which otherwise you might not have.

Finally, before going on to the next chapter to consider physical options as a way of responding to violence, I must stress how important it is for anyone who is a victim of abuse or violence, verbal or physical, to attempt to resolve the situation and its consequences to her own satisfaction, not someone else's. If you are still upset or disturbed about an incident after it is over, it is a good idea to seek counselling, or find someone whom you feel you can talk to at work or at home about what happened and how you feel about it. No single act of physically responding to violence can be a complete answer in itself; it can only be part of the appropriate solution.

3 Physical Responses to Violence

Any physical response to violence involves contact with a human body, and it is important, before contemplating such an option, that you should be aware of the various points on the body that are particularly sensitive or vulnerable.

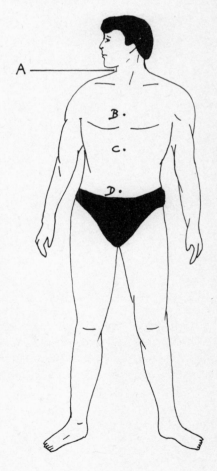

The human body is a mass of nerves and vital points, many of which are used for the purposes of acupuncture. Some of these points can be beneficial to health if treated, for example by an acupuncturist, but some can cause extreme pain or even death if hit or just pushed. It is not always necessary to strike a blow at these vital points, as firm pressure can also have the desired effect; it depends how seriously you view your situation. Are you being grabbed by someone who is fooling around, when you would prefer that they didn't, or are you being attacked by a dangerous aggressor? Point A is the Adam's apple. B is the point midway in the chest (this is a vulnerable point if struck hard). Point C is also potentially dangerous and point D is the belly button, below which no one can develop muscle, in and around the area of the bladder. A push here is as good as a strike.

In this illustration point A responds in a positive way if gently rubbed; people often rub this area to relieve their own stress or tension. But if this point is hit or struck it can have a very debilitating effect. Point B is the area we associate with loss of sensation in the leg, and C is a sensitive area, particularly if kicked, as is point D on the shin.

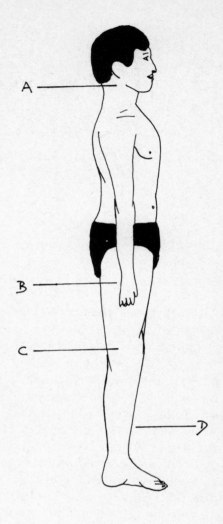

Looking at the head, point A responds to both a strike and a push, as it is a very sensitive area. Point B at the top of the head is a dangerous area to strike.

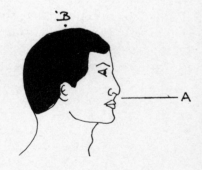

Here, points A and B can be rubbed or pushed with effect without causing lasting damage, which is not the case if they are hit. If you do push these points, try to use the thumbs, in a twisting motion, where the jaw meets the skull.

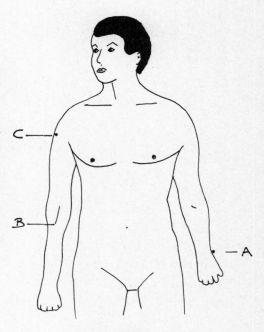

Points A, B and C on the body are all sensitive to being grabbed or to having fingers or thumbs pushed into them. Such actions are usually enough to make the most ardent attacker let go, unless of course he is in a frenzy, which must never be misunderstood. Everyone has a different pain threshold, and what may have an effect on one person may be ineffective on another. If you are in a physical situation you must try not to give up. If at first you don't succeed . . .

This illustration highlights the vulnerable areas of the neck and elbow, which again can be as effectively dealt with by a push as by a strike.

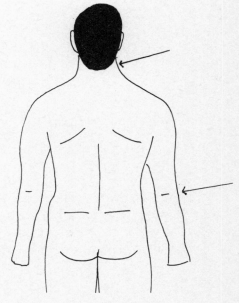

When going for the hand, it is most useful to target the thumb rather than the whole hand, particularly in the case of women who are being assaulted by someone stronger than themselves. Your attacker's whole hand will probably be stronger than yours, but it is unlikely that his thumb will be stronger than your hand.

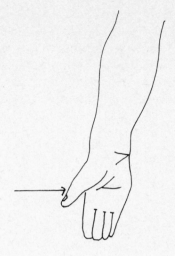

The arrowed area of the foot is the most effective place to stamp on, particularly if you are wearing spiked heels.

From a physical point of view, the two most important aspects of yourself for concern are your breathing and your balance. Fear, trepidation or panic can have a detrimental effect on either or both of them.

Usually, the first sensation you experience when under this kind of pressure is a sudden tightening of the chest and a loss of oxygen. This is a natural process, depriving you of up to 70 per cent of your usual amount. You don't really lose it, of course, as you actually have more flowing around your body, but you lose the use of it, unless you can find the even breathing pattern so necessary to get yourself moving, as opposed to being rooted to the spot. The first thing you must do is breathe deeply, down to the stomach, past the chest, making your stomach big and lowering your centre of gravity. You can practise this time and again when you are on your own, since practice makes perfect. The problem arises because usually the first thing you do when physically threatened is rise up and straighten your legs, when you ought to be lowering your centre of gravity and bending your legs for greater mobility, thus allowing you to move on the balls of your feet rather than with your heels flat on the ground. The illustrations below show the right and wrong postures to adopt. Try if you can to avoid the posture on the left.

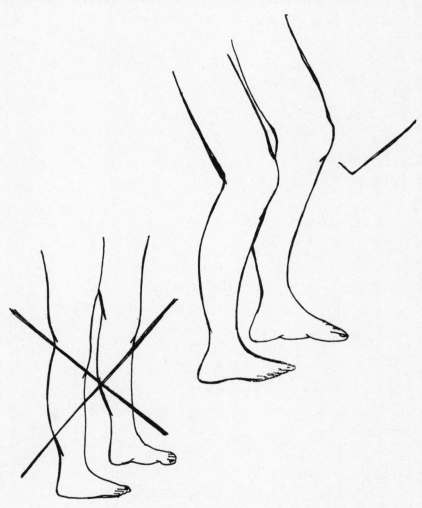

Whilst it may be extremely unpleasant to have to think about the possibility of being grabbed or held, there are several alternatives to physical action which you should bear in mind. We discussed one of them in the previous chapter—screaming at the very top of your voice, with as little warning as possible. The sheer surprise may make your attacker let go and, if his intentions were not serious, will create enough embarrassment for you to recover the initiative.

Another is to go completely limp, like a rag doll, which may suit your personality in a different way. Obviously there is always the possibility that this might go wrong, as your attacker might take an even tighter grip of you. But in practice you may have to try a range of alternatives if your first choice does not work.

WRIST GRABS

Let us look at a situation which could be placed in the Blue category.

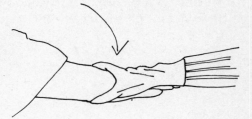

Your attacker has seized your right hand with his, in a wrist grab, reaching across your body. He has a strong grip and won't let go.

Don't struggle. Place your left hand over his right hand, pressing down firmly on top.

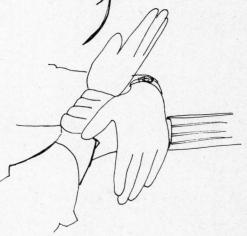

Twist your right hand back towards yourself, raising it slightly, still keeping a grip with the other hand.

55

Then twist your right hand back towards him, bringing it down into contact with your left wrist. It will touch a nerve in his wrist which produces an instant reaction. If he does not let go, just press down. If he still won't let go his wrist will break, so be careful.

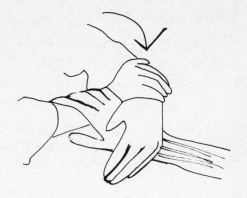

The sequence of breathing during this operation is very important. When you are first grabbed you should breathe deeply, right down into your stomach.

Keeping your breathing even and unhurried, breathe out as you raise and twist your right hand towards yourself.

Finish the exhalation of air in time with the last, decisive movement.

As I have already said, the physical attacks which come under the Blue category can, by virtue of their consequences, come under the Red category as well. We shall look at some of the others in the following pages.

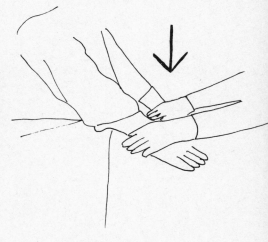

Your wrists are grabbed from the front. You simply breathe in, lower your weight and thrust your wrists downwards in one fluid movement, which should result in the freeing of your wrists. It is important to keep your back straight, your head up and your eyes focused on the area just in front of you.

Your right wrist is grabbed.

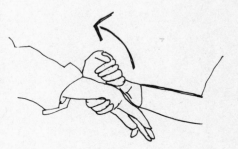

You reach over with your left hand and grab his thumb . . .

. . . and twist it back to the left. If you do it in one fluid movement, no injury will occur. If you jerk it, the thumb will break.

Some people argue from personal experience that, just by looking very hard at someone and making him the focus of their attention, they have stopped him attacking them. This, however, would require a great degree of composure, concentration and poise and a deep inner belief in your ability.

When your wrist is grabbed, you breathe in, then out, then in again as you grab your attacker's thumb, then out again as you twist it back.

Good balance is important throughout these movements, as is an awareness of where your feet are pointed. Sometimes, when you are under attack, your feet end up pointing in different directions, upsetting your balance. The simple rule is to have your feet facing in the same direction as your body, and if you wish to move in a different direction, point your feet there first; it makes it easier for the rest of your body to follow. At the same time keep your knees bent and fluid in your movements around the area of the lower body.

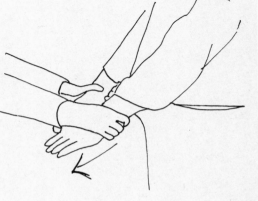

Your wrists are grabbed from the front. You open your fingers, pointed downwards.

Then you quickly turn your hands towards your attacker's thumbs (the line of
least resistance) and jerk your arms up-
wards, breaking his grip.

The breathing pattern for this sequence is that you breathe in quickly
when you are grabbed, then evenly breathe out as you open your fingers.
Then you breathe in again and breathe out as you turn your hands and jerk
your arms up.

GRABBED FROM BEHIND

You are grabbed from behind, round the throat. You cannot see your assailant. Without trying to look behind you, bring your head straight back—this will make him thrust his lower body towards you, even if you miss his face with your head.

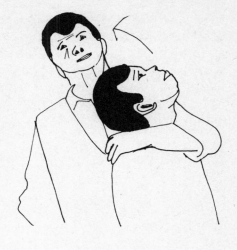

Then strike with your open hand, or grab, his groin.

Finally stamp down hard on the top of his foot.

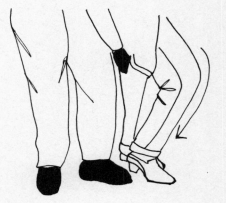

59

This is all one continuous movement. The actual contact matters less than the struggle you are putting up. You only have to make contact once, to try to get away.

You breathe in as soon as you get a chance when you are grabbed and try to breathe out as you bring your head back. Then breathe in again, then out as you reach for your attacker's groin, then in again, then out as you stamp on his foot.

SOMEONE ON TOP OF YOU

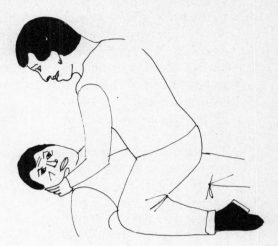

You are on the ground, and your attacker is on top of you, with his hands round your throat.

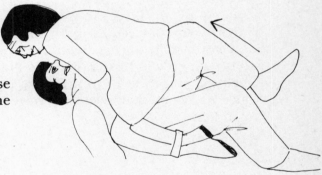

Bring your knee up, sharply into the base of his spine, breathe in as soon as he loosens his grip.

Then reach all the way round over his head, to his right ear, where the hair meets the face. Grab what you can and pull and twist him off you, breathing out at the same time.

61

There is a range of statistics targeted on specific types of profession which suggest that males are more likely to be subjected to attacks than females, but these concentrate on serious offences and tend to disregard verbal or physical assaults which they do not consider serious. Moreover, the professions studied tend to be those in which male employees predominate, so obviously any research would highlight the likelihood of men, rather than women, being attacked.

Women are usually considered an easy target, particularly in the workplace where they may be perceived as having a more vulnerable professional role. The first steps towards addressing this have their roots in the areas we covered in chapter 1, pp. 21–3.

If, however, you are unfortunate enough to be the victim of an assault, be careful not to be cast in the role of 'victim' by everyone around you for longer than is necessary. This promotes the idea that somehow you have done something wrong by being the subject of an attack, whether verbal or physical.

You are not in the wrong and distinctions must be drawn between any mistakes or misjudgements you may or may not have made, and short-comings in relation to the physical surroundings or safety at work pro-cedures which may be the real reason why you were targeted as a subject for assault by an assailant.

One way of preparing for such incidents is to get actively involved in pursuits such as yoga, which concentrate on the concept of an inner centre with which you harmonise. Meditation skills can be surprisingly useful in helping you to keep calm in the face of overwhelming pressure, and most alternative medicine centres have information about classes or groups you can join.

HAIR-PULLING

Hair-grabbing is an all too frequent occurrence, both for men and women. Whether your hair is short or long, the technique is the same: you press your head against the fingers and hand of the assailant, causing considerable pain, discomfort or, if you must, serious injury.

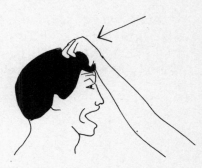

Your hair is grabbed from the front.

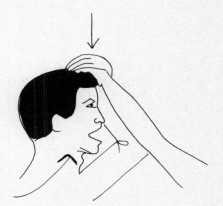

Place your hand on top of your assailant's and press up with your head and against your own hand, keeping his hand sandwiched between your head and your hand. Drop your head forward slightly and . . .

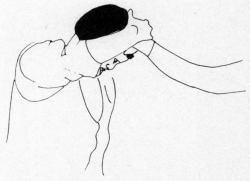

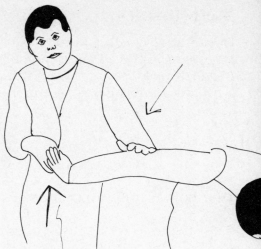

. . . twist very fast all the way round to your right (if he attacked and grabbed with his right hand. If he attacked with his left, you would eventually spin to your left).

Breathe in as you press your head against your attacker's hand, out as you drop your head, then breathe in and out as you spin round and free yourself.

This time your hair is grabbed from the back. You do exactly the same as before: put your hand on top of your attacker's, push, twist and . . .

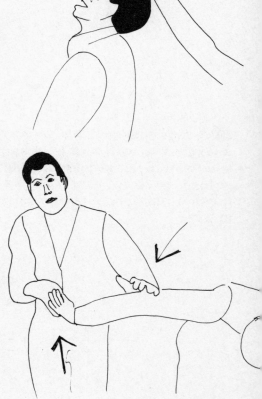

. . . turn in a circle to your right, if necessary keeping a firm grip on the assailant's wrist and elbow. It's up to you, although if it were me I'd be off!

Breathe as you are grabbed then breathe out as you turn, keeping the edge of your hand pressed into the vulnerable point at the attacker's elbow, with his wrist bent.

COPING WITH DANGEROUS ATTACKS

When you are grabbed round the throat or held by the hair and someone attempts to bang your head against the wall, then obviously serious injury or death may occur. It really doesn't take much to be seriously injured. Even if people do not intend to hurt you, the outcome is often tragically different from the intention.

There have been many incidents of people dying after being hit with only one blow, so you really haven't got the luxury of hoping that you will be all right if someone is attacking your throat or head. The human body is basically not designed to suffer great physical trauma caused by attack.

The wrist grabs are equally appropriate if you are attacked by someone wielding a weapon, but remember that if one of you receives a cut, whether it is you or the person who is attacking you, then blood makes the limbs slippery and getting a grip may be far more difficult.

Whether or not you choose to use a weapon to defend yourself is your decision. But if you feel your life is in danger, this may be the only choice open to you, assuming that it is impossible to run away or escape, which are the best possible choices. If you can, try to avoid tackling anyone with a weapon, but unfortunately it is not always that simple. If your life is in danger and you feel you need a weapon, a simple bunch of keys or a pen or a letter opener are usually the nearest things to hand.

Don't try to threaten with your weapon. If you are going to pick it up, use it, otherwise leave well alone. This is the one case where just threatening the other person is likely to make matters worse. Time spent threatening to do something is better spent in making a get-away. If there is a panic button in the office, use it. It does no harm to scream as well if you have the breath in your body, but don't be surprised if you try to scream and nothing comes out.

Finally, remember that once the heat of the moment is past and the cold light of reality takes over, other people may not take the same view as you with regard to 'reasonable force', so be prepared to argue your case after the event, particularly as facts may come to light, which at the time were not available to you.

The following sequence relates to a situation which one could put in the Red category, of the possibility of serious injury or even death.

Someone puts his hands round your throat, from the front.

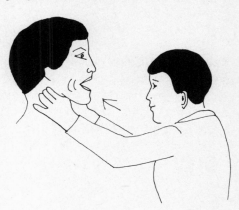

Remembering to breathe in, drop your weight, bend your knees and place your right hand, fingers straight, in your attacker's throat, keeping your arm bent.

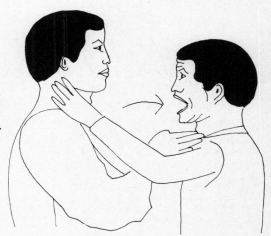

Then, straightening your arm, breathe out and turn away as his grip breaks, then run away!

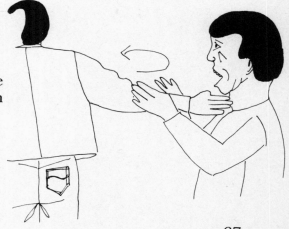

67

Here is one last example of how to deal with a serious attack.

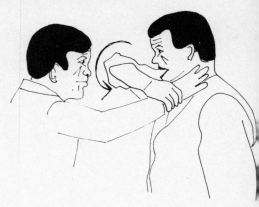

You are attacked from the front. The assailant holds you with both hands round the throat. You reach over and grip his right wrist with your right hand, breathing in and raising your right elbow at the same time . . .

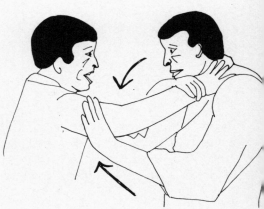

. . . then bring your right elbow down sharply into the crook of his left elbow. At the same time breathe out and bring your left hand up sharply into the point just behind his right elbow and . . .

. . . twist to your right and all the way round, keeping a grip on his wrist, until you are sure you are out of danger!

You cannot always know whether you are exposed to risk, or whether there is a likelihood of serious attack in your workplace, but it does no harm to be prepared for the possibility of being abused, verbally intimidated and physically attacked.

The British Crime Survey of 1988 concentrated on the risk of crime in the workplace: 'Workers said that a quarter of violent offences and over a third of threats they experienced were due to the work they did. A full half of threats against women were said to be job related . . . Welfare workers and nurses reported comparatively high levels of violence and threats due to their job.'*

The resultant fear, anger and stress which one may feel after being the victim of an assault are very serious. But too often women in particular are seen as natural victims by virtue of their gender. This must not be accepted practice. If you are attacked or abused by someone in the course of your work, do not allow the suggestion to creep in that by being female you somehow contributed to your attack. It is not always easy to do this, I know, but nevertheless it is worth being aware of this kind of culture as sometimes it operates it a very underhand and unclear way, so that you can even end up doubting your own feelings and start thinking that maybe you did contribute to your assault, just by being who you are. This is not fair and you must remember that.

*From the *British Crime Survey, 1988*, by Pat Mayhew, David Elliott and Lizanne Dowds. Home Office Research Study no. 111. London: HMSO.

4 People with a Disability

People with a disability are often subjected to verbal and physical assault as they are perceived as an 'easy target' or are viewed as somehow different from people classified as 'able-bodied'.

It is a mistake to think that because someone has a visible disability he or she will somehow be afforded more lenient treatment by people committing verbal or physical assault. There is little to support this notion.

People who lead their lives with a disability are just as likely to be attacked as an able-bodied person. Indeed, in some settings they are more likely to be targeted, possibly because of the nature of their job which may bring them into contact with people who are already at the very edge of their patience and who see a person with a disability as, somehow, a symbol of their frustration. There may also be a convention in some work settings that important 'clients' and issues are dealt with by able-bodied people and less important areas are given to employees with a disability. This is unacceptable but does happen.

There are times when you may be subjected to physical assault when you are in a seated position, such as a wheelchair.

You are seated and someone grabs you from behind, round the neck.

If you are in a wheelchair, slip the brakes on if you get a chance, breathe in when you can and . . .

. . . reach up and bend your assailant's thumb down, sharply towards you, trying to breathe out as you do so.

Obviously, there are other options open to you. If you are in a wheelchair, there is always the footrest, which would probably result in serious injury so should be used with caution, unless of course you have one which is padded.

Not everyone who has a disability is in a wheelchair, but regardless of your physical or mental ability you have an absolute right to defend yourself and also the right not to be classed as a victim just because of your perceived level of ability.

5 Implications for Workers and Clients

If a very serious and violent physical attack takes place, such as one with an offensive weapon, it is not fair for a worker to be expected to operate in a client-worker relationship again, nor is it realistic, particularly if a court case results from such an attack.

Sometimes employers frown upon the idea of a worker taking criminal proceedings against a client, but at the end of the day you have rights, like anyone else, as a citizen. Do not be less than honest, however, in your dealings with your employer. Just because he may not want you to take proceedings does not mean that he has no right to be told exactly what is going on.

Many assaults, whilst serious in that they simply should not have happened in the first place, do not involve serious physical violence. In these cases there is often an expectation by your employer, or even the client, that you should continue as before, in a worker-client relationship, putting the incident behind you.

There is something to be said for healing and growing from the pain you may have experienced, but I myself am very wary of the culture that suggests you have a responsibility to take up where you left off as a worker. This tends to be dictated by the setting of your work, particularly in social work. In fact, in my opinion social work is one of the main culprits in this type of collusive and unrealistic approach to the problem.

A police officer would not be expected to deal with an individual on a personal level if there was the possibility of proceedings taking place between them, and likewise in the nursing profession a conflict of interest tends to be recognised.

In the social work world, however, everything is rather blurred in relation to the aftermath of assaults and violence to staff. In the area offices, where social workers known as field workers tend to have their base, there is generally a work-style environment, with secretarial assistance, individual offices or open plan offices (where space is at a premium). There will be a set pattern of hierarchy from one manager to another, down to the individual social workers. Each social worker carries what is known as a caseload, which basically means a collection of individual clients whom she will be expected to meet and support in their everyday life problems.

Overlapping with this are specific types of work which involve particular aspects of the law, such as child protection and mental health work, where the frequency of contact and style of work are not really open to individual interpretation but are a matter of law. These elements can and do blur the edges for social workers when it comes to violence from clients.

If a worker is assaulted by a parent of a child who is the subject of a child protection order, it can be very difficult simply to transfer the case; the appropriate level of social worker may not be available, or it may be felt that the worker who has been assaulted has too detailed a knowledge of the family just to cease working with them because she has been assaulted. Whilst I understand this approach to the problem, I do think it unfair towards the individual social worker, as it tends to disregard her feelings and creates an atmosphere which can make it difficult for her to say how scared or apprehensive she may be feeling. This is where the quality of the individual manager is crucial.

A good manager will recognise the worker's feelings and respect her for them, rather than attempt to put pressure on her to behave in a certain way. The relationship between manager and worker will inevitably have been affected by a violent incident and it is important to get any feelings aired and examined.

If it is considered appropriate for a worker to carry on with an individual or a family despite having been assaulted, provision must be made to ensure that a similar event cannot occur again, even if this means offending the sensibilities of the individuals or family concerned. This is very important, as it undermines the worker if she or he feels that the client is being given full consideration and the worker none at all. Obviously this may not be the case, but it may well be how the worker sees it, on top of any other feelings such as anger, guilt, stress or fear, which are all quite natural.

The office style of environment which exists in social work area offices makes it possible to create a safe barrier to support the worker in subsequent dealings with a particular client. This, of course, only works if everyone is aware of the situation. It doesn't work if people have different perceptions of what information should or should not be passed on.

One area office I worked in gave me an unpleasant experience which I won't forget in a hurry. One of my clients was a powerful young man who appeared to hate the world and everyone in it. I made a decision, affecting his life, which did not please him, so he came down to the office one day with a large piece of wood and declared his intention of inserting it in me in the most violent fashion.

I was not there at the time as it was my day off, but the member of staff who dealt with him duly gave him the exact day, time and place when I would be back on duty! This is a good example of how not to do it. Whilst he may have had a right to know, as a client, when I would be back at work, he had forfeited that right, in my opinion, by declaring his intention to damage me. He could not have it both ways. People cannot threaten other individuals physically and continue in the fantasy that this will not affect future dealings with them.

At the same time the message which the incident gave to me was not a very supportive one. I began to feel unsafe even when I was not at work. These are the kinds of feelings that have to be tackled, with the client if necessary, but at the same time a firm overview must be held by the worker and manager.

Discussions or meetings about an assault on a member of staff, no matter how serious, should not turn into a learning experience for the benefit of the client. This is simply not fair to the worker. There are formats for people to explore the violence within them—attacking a worker and then being able to have a chat about it afterwards is not the correct way to proceed. It gives the wrong message to both worker and client. This is not to deny that the person who committed the assault can learn from it. If that happens in the course of proceedings, all well and good, but that should not be the sole aim of discussions and work involving everyone after the event.

Apart from the area offices, there are many establishments up and down the country, run by local authority social work departments and private agencies, which offer residential support to a wide range of clients, from teenagers to elderly people and those who are mentally ill. They are staffed by workers who operate a shift system, which usually includes senior and qualified workers. This type of work has made headlines in the national press due to a number of scandals, but the general public has no clear idea of what life is like for residents and workers, despite the in-depth studies carried out by national newspapers after each fresh story comes to light.

Most of the attention has concentrated on the abuse suffered by individuals in certain homes, at the hands of workers. Obviously these are terrible cases which should never have happened, but they are usually the result of poor supervision, management and monitoring procedures rather than pure human wickedness operating on its own.

What is not commonly realised or understood, except by the residents and workers themselves, is the reality of actually working and living in an institution.

Unlike the office environment, if assault or violence occurs in a residential establishment, the people involved still have to deal with each other, unless one or more parties are removed from the setting. This may happen if an official inquiry takes place into a serious allegation of improper conduct, or a resident is clearly out of control and a risk to himself or others. But more often than not some very serious assaults are made on staff by residents and nothing at all is done to sort out the problem.

The reasons for this vary, but the most common is a general uncertainty about the possible options, as well as the prevailing tendency to blame the staff first and the resident second, even though facts and circumstances may suggest otherwise.

Many staff are afraid that they will be out of a job if they make a complaint, or feel that they will be seen as the problem and that the solution will be for them to leave. Sometimes the reason can be traced to inexperienced or short-sighted managers. I hesitate to make too much of an issue over training, as many of the people who have been at the centre of some of the national scandals have been well trained.

Managers in these settings, however, would certainly benefit from training in ways of dealing with the aftermath of violence in a residential institution.

It is interesting to note that the Central Council for Education and Training in Social Work (CCETSW) does not carry any national training initiatives in relation to violence at work. This may well be because it is not expected to, but the question remains: just where do people go to receive the appropriate level of training, on a national basis, in dealing with violence at work? Most of the effective responses seem to be at a local level, where individual departments have taken an initiative and set up training for their staff, concentrating on various aspects of dealing with violence.

The basic point is that when it comes to violence there are no winners, just a greater number of frightened and confused individuals, all of whom need help and support at work.

In conclusion, it must be realised that violence and assault should not be confused with the controversy about restraining in children's homes. At the time of writing a debate is raging about appropriate levels of restraint which should be used towards young people in council-run homes. It is an important and vital debate but has nothing to do with assault and violence at work, unless of course that is what restraint becomes in any given situation.

6 Support and Instruction in the Workplace

It is all about choices, and being clear about which ones you are able to make.

A nurse in the health services got into trouble for responding to serious racial abuse and intimidation from a recipient of the service she was supposed to be providing. Eventually, in cases like that, it becomes clear that if you cannot be true to yourself, you cannot be true to the people you are trying to help. The nurse made her choice and stood bravely by it, but it is also worth considering that in certain issues, like that of race, some people have no choice but to make a stand: they have nowhere to run, so they must face up to it. Someday that could be you or me.

There are departments and councils which attempt, to their credit, to monitor and evaluate the frequency of abuse and attacks against their staff, but often the forms designed to record such incidents are not returned, because people do not think there is any point. Believe me, there is a point. The less a subject is discussed and considered the more the face-to-face worker has to deal with it, and opportunities for dialogue and consideration of the problems should not be missed.

Hertfordshire is one local authority that issues guidelines to its staff, and attempts to address the issues. In its 'Staff Guidelines on Violence by Clients' it states, 'all people have the right in law to use reasonable force to protect themselves, to protect others and to protect property. What is reasonable depends on all the circumstances but will be the minimum force necessary to bring about protection. Staff should never meet violence with violence.'

What is violence, what is reasonable and what is safe and for whom? At the end of the day it is the face-to-face worker who has to make that decision, often in isolation. Clearly, this should not be the case, but it invariably is.

However, the responsibility for bringing about change in individual work settings comes down to the managers and supervisors who work there.

They have a responsibility to their workers to help create an environment which is safe and healthy for everyone concerned, and by doing so they recognise the responsibility of the organisation to take into account the situations in which violence occurs and the effects these incidents have on their staff.

Firstly, they have to be fully aware of the boundaries and restrictions in place because of the work setting. Thus if it is not possible to move residents from one home to another purely on the basis of their perceived level of aggression and potential for violence, then all the workers should know this. It is the responsibility of the manager to ensure that all his or her workers know about the constraints and boundaries governing them all, including the manager.

Support is all about honesty and caring about what happens to your staff. Many of the techniques described and illustrated in this book are easily learnt and, once grasped, passed on to other workers for their benefit. You do not have to be an 'expert' to allow someone else to share your experience and grasp of a subject. Obviously, without an understanding of the limitations and realities involved in the work of dealing with the public in vulnerable situations, the movements on their own are simplistic and isolated, but taken against the backdrop of the work setting they can be appropriate and a useful tool for learning.

The colour categories of Green, Yellow, Blue and Red can be discussed, the different priorities agreed and the appropriate responses written down in the form of a contract. Then if a situation occurs which is considered to be a 'Yellow' one, a certain course of action will be followed by everyone, not just by one or two individuals on their own.

It is the manager's responsibility to make sure that there is unity of purpose and clarity of aim in everything that takes place in the work setting, and that includes responses to violence and aggression towards members of his staff. At the same time he should make sure that managers and supervisors above him in the line of command are kept informed of what he is doing and how he is doing it, and why. It should not be left until something actually happens before others are informed about a system for responding to a problem of a violent nature. When the manager takes responsibility for this, a culture of co-operation is created for the common good.

Professional counselling must also be available, as and when required, for staff who experience violence at work, since the effects are often very long-term. No one is the same—some people take only a short while to get over the effects, whilst others may take much longer.

What is absolutely sure is that without help, support, counselling where appropriate and managerial supervision the chances of anyone getting over the effects of violence and aggression are actually quite slim. The following is an example of one kind of initiative which a manager can take. It is a synopsis of a course on aggression and violence and how to cope and is an indicator for managers to follow, should they so wish.

FORMAT FOR A COURSE

The course was attended by social workers from both field and residential backgrounds, with a variety of client groups. It carried the title 'Managing Aggression'.

The work was undertaken in one large group involving all participants and in four small groups, at specific times during the course. Each time the large group reconvened after being split into four, there was a feedback session when the individual topics discussed were presented to the large group by a spokesperson for each small group.

During the two days of the course, the following main issues were covered:

1   The origins and process of aggression, conflict and violence.
2   The nature of the professional relationship of social worker and client.
3   Supervision, support and communication—their role in creating and solving conflict.
4   The important differences between aggression, conflict and violence and the way they manifest themselves in the work setting—field and residential.
5   The role of the police and the law and social work.
6   Practical ways of responding, or not responding, to violence.
7   Simple and advanced methods of relaxation.

This short summary aims to give an overview of the course and is not meant to be a description of each group session. Nor is it intended to describe what the participants thought about the sessions. It is merely a factual account of the areas covered.

The aim of the course was to examine the nature of aggression in the social work setting and to highlight the problems of preserving one's physical and mental well-being, whilst at the same time acknowledging that the client-social worker relationship is unique. Defending oneself against physical threat from a client is quite different from responding to threat, physical or otherwise, from other sources. Added to this is the fact that inflicting physical harm on another human being, regardless of the justification, is extremely hard to do, and it can help to know one's own boundaries before certain situations are experienced.

The practical sessions highlighted the difficulty of physical action and concentrated on allowing people the experience of facing threat from another individual, in a safe setting. 'Self-Defence' involves the striking or grappling of another human being and the problems inherent in this were highlighted by the use of an air-filled bag which course members were allowed the

81

opportunity to hit. Striking an inanimate object which felt no pain was quite difficult for many participants and underlined the weakness of conventional approaches to self-defence, which make no allowance for individuals' inhibitions about physical action, particularly against a client, dangerous or otherwise.

The participants identified the essential elements in the professional setting as quality supervision and support from fellow-workers, as well as the harnessing of individual's professional experience. They felt that conflict and aggression, and ultimately violence, often took place as a direct result of lack of one or all of these elements.

The important differences between, conflict, aggression and violence were basically identified in the following way: Conflict was seen as something which need not always be negative, and can in fact be used in a positive way in a controlled environment—it is possible for people to agree to differ and can be healthy, even though it may also be viewed as wrong in certain circumstances. It was also seen as something which can bring about change. Participants felt that the role of the social worker may create conflict by the use of authority and also as a result of other people's perceptions of authority. Social workers are at the mercy of government policy and may be victims of the general public's frustrations. The problems of duty-work and late visits, particularly by females alone, were seen as great sources of concern and potential situations for conflict.

Aggression was generally seen as negative, although some participants felt that it could sometimes be useful, but only if dealt with by someone experienced and confident in this type of 'face-to-face' situation. It was seen as a loss of control, not a gain, and potentially very threatening, often leading to physical violence itself.

Violence was seen as the ultimate loss of control and the one thing which people generally felt they had little answer to. Once it started there was little to do but hope for a successful outcome. Understanding the process could help to avert it, but not always, and the practical aspects of the course lent themselves most readily to this facet of the problems encountered in professional social work.

The process of conflict, aggression and violence was seen as a circular one, often created by the social work task. It is circular causation and can start at any point.

The social worker as a victim was considered in that social workers often absorb pain and distress as well as being the scapegoat for social ills. A feeling of frustration and powerlessness on the part of the client group, coupled with traditional problems of communication, is an added ingredient in this mixture.

The control of problem areas was identified as having its roots in the quality of the client-worker relationship, and this was where poor case notes, handovers and bad supervision caused most problems. It could infect the quality of the client-worker relationship and in itself led to potential for conflict and violence.

The role of the police, police assistance and the perceptions of magistrates were examined, and it was generally felt that the quality of support or understanding for the social work task depended largely on individual police officers and forces. The general perception was that magistrates were unaware of the intricate nature of social work and that if this state of affairs was to improve there would have to be joint courses for social workers, magistrates and police. The topic of procedure within individual departments was considered in relation to professional and legal support when a worker is assaulted and intends to take criminal proceedings against an individual. If an individual department is supportive there is generally no problem, even though ignorance of workers' rights and right to advice can still prevail. It is when workers are left on their own that tremendous problems of confidence and professional isolation can arise.

The feedback sessions gave the course members the opportunity to share each other's perceptions in a formal but relaxed way, and the general feeling at the end of the course was a positive one: people felt they had learnt and experienced something of use. Violence and the process of conflict and aggression leading up to it are not pleasant or attractive professional prospects, but they occupy a prominent position in the personal social services. These elements will not go away, but if they are approached in the correct manner and understood for what they are, then the job, role and ultimate personal survival of the social worker in modern times can be improved and enhanced in a professional and acceptable way.

7 Conclusion

All victims of violence are eligible to make a claim from the Criminal Injuries Compensation Board, providing the incident has been reported to the police.

The perpetrator need not have been identified or arrested or convicted for the Board to make an award, but the process can be lengthy due to the obvious need to check the facts and circumstances of each individual case, and because the Board deals with many applications, all of which receive individual consideration.

Remember, however, if you are a victim of violence whilst at work, that each employer can have a different attitude to courses of action such as calling the police or making applications to the Board. It is best to be sure about his position before an incident occurs, so that you can be certain where you stand.

Violence in the workplace is unique. It is not the same as experiencing it at home or in the street. There are restrictions and, as we have seen, if the violence is perpetrated by someone you are supposed to be working with or for, it is far from easy to know exactly what to do or how to respond in a given situation.

Having read this book, are you now ready to take on every situation involving violence or aggression at work—solving it quickly and easily for the benefit of all? Of course not—that is not possible. No one can go it alone, and that is the whole point of this book. It is meant to provide you with assistance and guidance and, most importantly of all, to assure you that when it comes to violence and aggression and the effect it has on you—you are not alone!

Dirk Robertson
Hertfordshire, 1993

Useful Addresses

Criminal Injuries Compensation Board
19–30 Alfred Place, London WC1E 7EA. Tel: 071-636 9501

London Buses Ltd, Public Relations Office
172 Buckingham Palace Road, London SW1W 9TN. Tel: 071-918 3054

Metropolitan Police Headquarters
Telephone enquiries only: 071-230 1212

National Association of Victim Support Schemes
Cranmer House, 39 Brixton Road, London SW9 6DZ. Tel: 071-735 9166

National Institute for Social Work
Mary Ward House, 5 Tavistock Place, London WC1H 9SN. Tel: 071-387 9681

Royal College of Nursing
20 Cavendish Square, London W1M 9AE. Tel: 071-409 3333

UNISON
1 Mabledon Place, London WC1H 9AJ. Tel: 071-388 2366

Further Reading

New Committee set up to examine violence to staff. In *Social Service Insight*, 5.12.86, p.4. (Reports on the announcement by the Secretary of State.)

Braithwaite, R. Coming to terms with the effects of violence. In *Social Work Today*, 20.10.88, pp.19–20. (Offers suggestions, based on practical experience, of how to handle the complex and long-lasting effects on social workers who have been the victims of a violent attack.)

Braithwaite, R. Training for trouble. In *Community Care*, 27.7.89, pp.23–4. (Kingston-upon-Thames SSD followed up an internal survey identifying the scale of violence faced by their social workers with a training package.)

Braithwaite, R. Running away is OK. In *Social Work Today*, 23.4.92, pp.22–3. (Offers techniques for coping with violent confrontations with clients.)

Britton, J. Care staff are most at risk from violence. In *Care Weekly*, 21.10.88, p.2. (Reports on a survey of staff in children's centres and homes for the mentally handicapped.)

Clare, P. Post Traumatic Stress Disorder: offender, victim and colleague as survivors. In *Probation Journal*, December 1992, pp.175–80. (Argues that insights offered by a closer understanding of PTSD can enhance probation practice, particularly in fulfilling the demands of the Criminal Justice Act 1991, and in responding to the needs of colleagues who are the victims of violence at work.)

Clode, D. Recipe for reducing risks. In *Social Services Insight*, 13.3.87, pp.6–7. (Summarises a draft of guidelines on dealing with violence produced by the ADSS)

Cohen, P. Nightmare on work street. In *Social Work Today*, 23.4.92, pp.21–2. (Reports on responses to a stabbing incident in a Leeds SSD area office.)

Crate, R. Social workers and violent clients: management response. In *Social Work Today*, 10.11.86, pp.14–15. (Survey of management guidelines.)

Downey, R. Behind closed doors. In *Social Work Today*, 23.7.92, p.11. (A report from Victim Support has highlighted the need for governmental lead on the issue of domestic violence, and the crucial role that social workers have to play.)

Eccles, K., and Tutt, N. Defence of the realm. In *Social Services Insight*, 4.12.87, pp.16–18. (Describes a training programme used in a social services department to help staff to deal with violence.)

Francis, W. Under attack. In *Community Care* 13.11.86, pp.24–5. (Three social workers who were victims of attacks tell their stories.)

Francis, W. What the organisations say. In *Community Care* 4.12.86, pp.22–3. (Professional organisations' views on violence to social workers.)

Goddard, C., and Carew, B. Protecting the child: hostages to fortune? In *Social Work Today*, 15.12.88, pp.12–13. (The Stockholm Syndrome describes the paradoxical relationship that can develop between hostage and captor. In situations of threatened violence social workers can unconsciously act like hostages. Research has shown this to happen in child abuse cases.)

Hatchett, W. Getting to grips with aggression. In *Residential and Day Care Weekly*, 17.6.88, p.10. (Leeds SSD's workshops for residential and day care staff.)

Home, A. Responding to domestic violence: a comparison of social workers' and police officers' interventions. In *Social Work and Social Sciences Review*, 3(2), 1991–2, pp.150–62. (Research in Canada showed that social workers referred women more to shelters, social services and legal aid than police would. Police were more likely to intervene in cases of physical abuse rather than emotional abuse.)

Hopkins, J. Meeting the care needs of staff in the PSS. In *Social Work Today*, 16.11.87, pp.14–15. (Reviews a series of previous articles; with guidelines for self-help.)

Janner, G. The rough road to compensation. In *Social Work Today*, 17.8.89, p.22. (Considers the legal rights of social workers who have been assaulted.)

Johnson, S. Guidelines for social workers in coping with violent clients. In *British Journal of Social Work*, 18(4), August 1988, pp.377–90. (Reviews theories of aggression, discusses local authorities' attitudes, and the problem of assessing risk.)

King, J. How do you handle violence? In *Community Care* 23.3.89, pp.22–3. (The results of a Community Care survey into violence in social work—field, residential and management.)

Laurance, J. Social work and self-defence. In *New Society*, 5.12.86, pp.12–13. (Sums up recent evidence and research, particularly in Strathclyde.)

Littlechild, B. Addressing aggression. In *Community Care* 1.4.93, pp.20–1. (Policy dealing with violence to staff currently concentrates on how individual workers should recognise and defuse violent situations and in effect take responsibility for their clients' behaviour. Staff therefore fear that they will become double victims: of the initial incident, and of unsupportive employers. Argues for policies and training which acknowledge that all violent situations cannot be defused and calls for total staff involvement in creating strategies for dealing with prevention of violence and provision of support when the need arises.)

Lunn, T. Plea for staff protection. In *Community Care*, 14.4.88, p.9. (An 'early day motion' in the House of Commons has highlighted the problems of violence to social services staff.)

Lyons, K. *et al.* My brilliant career. In *Social Work Today*, 10.9.92, pp.14–15. (A pilot study by the University of East London has highlighted some areas of concern over the relevance of social work training to practice, violence, and stress.)

McDonnell, A. *et al.* Staff training in the management of violence and aggression. In *Mental Handicap*, 19(2) June 1991, pp.73–6. (Training is placed in the context of an organisational system; emphasises the need for clear policies and describes the process of specifying a training system.)

McHugh, J. Why violence against staff goes unreported. In *Social Work Today* 21.9.87, pp.9–10. (Reports on a recent survey of measures used by different social work agencies to combat violence against staff.)

McNeeney, T. A walk on the wild side. In *Community Care*, 15.3.90, pp.20–1. (Social workers in New York, and social services agencies, have a high awareness of self-protection. Armed security guards stand watch at most of the Human Resources Administration's offices.)

More, W. Effective training for worker safety. In *The Journal of Training and Development*, 1(4) 1991, pp.43–52. (Describes the theory of 'risk compensation' and the implication that staff training must start with awareness raising about risk in potentially violent situations.)

O'Hara, M. Fistful of power. In *Social Work Today*, 4.2.93. pp.18–19. (There is growing evidence that a high proportion of men who abuse their partners also physically abuse their children, and that children are profoundly affected by witnessing violence against their mothers whether or not they have been abused themselves. Highlights the effects on children and looks at what social workers can do to help.)

Phillips, R. and Leadbetter, D. Violent sessions in the classroom. In *Social Work Today*, 1.2.90, pp.22–3. (Stirling University has run a special course to prepare social work students for aggression from clients.)

Protherough, C. How social workers can cope with being victims. In *Social Work Today*, 21.9.87, pp.10–12. (Recounts the author's experience of being a victim of violence, and offers some practical advice for both victims and their colleagues, as well as family and friends.)

Pugh, P. How to build a system for managing violence. In *Social Work Today*, 1.9.88, pp.14–15. (Practical advice on how to control violence in residential and day care settings.)

Roman, D.D. and Annis, L.V. Behavioural and situational clues to a psychiatrist's murder by her brother. In *International Journal of Offender Therapy and Comparative Criminology*, 30(2), 1986, pp.177–82.

(Examines a case history for clues which would have helped to avoid a tragedy.)

Ross, M. and Glisson, C. Bias in social work intervention with battered women. In *Journal of Social Services Research*, 14(3/4) 1991, pp.79–105. (A study of a small sample of social workers indicated that social workers stereotype clients who have been battered, and that they are less likely to consider relocation as an option to protect the victim who is married to her attacker. Male social workers, surprisingly, focused on violence-related concerns as targets for intervention more than the female social workers.

Saunders, L. Safe and secure in Surrey? Violence to staff of the social services department. In *Social Services Research* no. 5/6 1987, pp.32–55. (Policy, procedures and training.)

Schwarz, V. Professionalism versus hindsight. In *Community Care* 11.8.88, pp.18–20. (Discusses the Inquiry Report into Isobel Schwarz's death.)

Schwarz, V. Social worker, heal thyself. In *Community Care* 8.1.87, pp.14–15. (Social workers who are victims of violent attacks have a capacity for accepting culpability, which allows management to be less than vigilant when it comes to preventative measures, claims the father of murdered social worker Isobel Schwarz.)

Small, N. Putting violence towards social workers into context. In *Critical Social Policy*, 7(1) 1987, pp.40–51.

Stevens, J. Healing the hidden wounds. In *Community Care*, 8.9.88, pp.22–3. (Relives the experience of being seriously attacked by a disturbed client, and the emotional aftermath.)

Tonkin, B. Quantifying risk factors. In *Community Care* 13.11.86, pp.22–3. (Gives evidence that violence to social workers has often been under-reported and gives some assessment of likely types of aggressor.)

Tonkin, B. Plan for a preventive policy. In *Community Care*, 11.12.86, pp.22–3. (Describes Strathclyde's scheme to prevent violent attacks on social workers.)

Tutt, N. Violence to staff. In *Practice*, 3(1), Spring 1989, pp.80–91. (Incidence, definition, prediction.)

Werner, P.D. *et al.* Social workers' decision-making about the violent client. In *Social Work Research and Abstracts*, 25(3), September 1989, pp.17–20. (A study of the cues used by social workers in assessing risk of violence in clients.)

Whiteley, P. A torturous task. In *Social Work Today*, 9.4.92, pp.14–15. (Reports on expertise built up by social workers in Chile with clients who have been victims of torture.)

Williams, B. Violence and risk at work. In *Probation Journal*, 35(4), December 1988, pp.135–6,139. (Although the Probation Service has been slower than Social Services in responding to the problem of violence by clients, detailed guidance is now available in some areas; gives examples of practice.)

Research References

All the items listed below are in the library of the National Institute for Social Work (see address p. 87).

Association of Directors of Social Services. (Guidelines and recommendations to employers on violence against employees. ADSS, 1987. 32pp.)

Birmingham. Social Services Department. Report of the Director of Social Services to the Social Services Committee: Aggression at work. Birmingham: Birmingham Social Services Department, 1988. 2pp, tables.

British Association of Social Workers. *Violence to social workers*. Birmingham: BASW, 1988. 72pp., bibliog. (Discusses issues for social work practice, management responsibilities and sets out guidelines for social work staff.)

Brown, R., Bute, S., Ford, P. *Social workers at risk: the prevention and management of violence*. Basingstoke: Macmillan/British Association of Social Workers, 1986. 145pp., tables, bibliog.

Cambridgeshire. Social Services Department. Management of violence at work: guidelines for social services staff. Cambridge: Cambridgeshire SSD, 1987. 9pp.

Crane, D. *Violence on social workers*. Norwich: University of East Anglia, 1986. 44pp., bibliog.

Dorset. Social Services Department. Dealing with violence: guidance to staff on violence by clients. Dorchester: Dorset SSD, 1988. 8pp. (A statement of intent by the County Council and guidelines for staff.)

Dudley. Social Services Department. Violence to staff: report of the departmental working party. Dudley: Dudley SSD., 1987. 35pp., tables.

Essex. Social Services Department. Violence at work: practice guidelines for social services staff. Chelmsford: Essex. Social Services Department, 1989. 28pp. (Guidelines exploring causes, prevention and reduction, and dealing with and anticipating violence. Discusses these in three workplace settings: residential and day care, hospitals, and area offices, giving clear guidelines and reporting procedure for each.

Great Britain. Department of Health and Social Security. Report of DHSS conferences on violence to staff. December 1986. London: DHSS, 1987. 20pp.

Great Britain. Department of Health and Social Security. *Report of the committee of inquiry into the care and aftercare of Miss Sharon Campbell.* Chair: John Spokes. London: HMSO, 1988. 92pp., (Cm 440). (The report into the murder of social worker Isobel Schwarz by a client.)

Great Britain. Department of Health and Social Security. *Violence to staff: Report of the DHSS Advisory Committee on violence to staff.* London: HMSO, 1988. 52pp. (Recommendations for policy and practice in dealing with violence.)

Kingston. Social Services Department. Coping with violence: the strategy. Kingston: Kingston Social Services Department. 1991. 27pp., tables. (Defines violence and states principles, procedures and policy for coping with it.)

Labour Research Department. Bargaining report no. 64, July 1987. Pages 5–12: 'Assaults on staff'. London: LRD, 1987. 15pp., tables.

Leicestershire. Social Services Department. Violence to staff. Leicester: Leicestershire SSD, 1988. 10pp. (Brief notes on the measures taken by the County Council for the prevention and management of violence, particularly within the Social Services Department.)

Local Government Management Board. *Violence at work: issues, policies and procedures.* Luton: Local Government Management Board, 1991. 79pp., tables, bibliog. (Focuses on two local authorities which have developed policies and procedures for dealing with violence to staff. Looks at the implementation of policy and the operation of procedures. Draws conclusions and makes recommendations, including the use of performance indicators to evaluate such programmes.)

More, W. *Aggression and violence: steps to safety at work.* Birmingham: Pepar, 1991. 47pp., bibliog. (Practical guidance for human services workers on managing difficult situations at work. Looks at understanding risk; understanding aggression by clients; and maintaining safety by avoiding potentially dangerous situations via minimising the client's frustration, being aware of potential triggers, dampening the spiralling process, and protecting yourself and escaping.)

Norris, D. *Violence against social workers: the implications for practice.* London: Jessica Kingsley, 1990. 176pp., tables, bibliog. (Surveys existing literature and research. Looks at attitudes of social workers and management response. Surveys current policy and practice based on questionnaires sent to all SSDs and Probation Departments. Recommends national minimum standards.

North Yorkshire. Social Services Department. Violence and aggression: guidance for social services staff. Northallerton: North Yorkshire SSD, 1990. 4pp. (Brief guidelines on preventing and dealing with violent situations, and counselling, insurance and legal advice available from the Department.)

Poyner, B. and Warne, C. Violence to staff: a basis for assessment and prevention. London: HMSO, 1986. 16pp., diags.

Poyner, B. and Warne, C. *Preventing violence to staff.* London: Health and Safety Executive, 1988. 81pp., tables, illus. (Discusses a framework for analysis, and includes a number of case studies, including Strathclyde Social Work Department's working group on violence to staff.)

Rowett, C. *Violence in social work: a research study of violence in the context of local authority social work.* Cambridge: University of Cambridge, Institute of Criminology, 1986. 158pp., tables, bibliog.

Smith, F. *An analysis of violence towards staff in a Social Services Department.* Fergus Smith, 1988. 70pp., tables. (Survey undertaken in Croydon to assess the extent and nature of the problem, with recommendations for future policy and practice.)

Strathclyde. Social Work Department. Violence to staff: policies and procedures. Glasgow: The Department, 1986. 35pp., appendices, bibliog.

Surrey County Council. Social Services Department. *Safe and secure in Surrey?—report of the social services working group on violence to staff.* Kingston upon Thames: Surrey. Social Services Department, 1987. 100pp., tables, diags., bibliog.

Surrey County Council. Social Services Department. 'Safe and secure in Surrey?'—research report of the working group on violence to staff. Kingston upon Thames: Surrey. Social Services Department, 1987. 41pp., tables.

Thomas, T. *The police and social workers.* Aldershot: Gower, 1986. 154pp. (Highlights areas of joint work and the difficulties experienced by these two occupational groups. Illustrates the guidelines that exist and suggests ways of improving the work that police and social workers do together. Clarifies work carried out in the areas of child abuse, mental disorder, domestic violence and juvenile offenders, and examines areas of common concern, such as community-orientated work and issues relating to the Police and Criminal Evidence Act 1984.